THE BEST OF
Billy Keane

For Care &
Kane,

Im John

B's

love

Billy

THE BEST OF
Billy Keane

*From a writer who sees
extraordinary deeds
in day-to-day living*

Ballpoint Press

*This book is dedicated to my brothers Conor and John
and my sister Joanna.*

Published in 2016 by Ballpoint Press
4 Wyndham Park, Bray, Co Wicklow, Republic of Ireland.
Telephone: 00353 86 821 7631
Email: ballpointpress1@gmail.com
Web: www.ballpointpress.ie

ISBN 978-0-9932892-2-4

While every effort has been made to ensure the accuracy of
all information contained in this book, neither the author
nor the publisher accepts liability for any errors or omissions made.

Book design and production by Joe Coyle Media&Design,
joecoyledesign@gmail.com

© Cover photographs by Mark Condren

Printed and bound by GraphyCems

Contents

CONTENTS

About The Author

BILLY KEANE is a publican and writer from Listowel, Co Kerry. He has been a columnist with the Irish Independent for 16 years.

Married with four children, Billy is the eldest son of Mary, who died last year, and John B, the legendary playwright and writer who died in 2002.

He is the author of two novels, *The Last of the Heroes* (2005) and *The Ballad of Mo & G* (2013). Billy has also co-written the late Moss Keane's autobiography, *Rucks, Mauls and Gaelic Football* and Billy Morgan's autobiography *Rebel, Rebel*.

Introduction

BILLY KEANE'S *Irish Independent* columns focus mostly on the lives of ordinary people as they go about their daily and weekly business.

He is a writer with a finger firmly on the pulse of the Ireland of today – examining various issues against a backdrop of old rituals and new norms before trying to make sense of it all for us.

Keane's pen is both sensitive and sympathetic as it probes the human condition, frailties and all, in its different guises.

His gift is that he can translate these stories with humour and observations that uplift and sustain, leaving readers in a better frame of mind after they finish reading his narrative of the day.

The author has also been a columnist for *The Kerryman* and has included some of his writing from that time.

1

Mam Picked Her Day To Meet Up Again With Dad, It Didn't Pick Her

First published: August 18, 2015

OUR mother is dressed up in her best by her friend Phil. And she has a lovely smile. It's the smile she keeps for Dad.

"She's herself," says Auntie Lena. The sickness is all gone from her now. Mam is happy.

They met up yesterday for The Fifteenth, Mam and Dad that is.

The 15th is the feast day of Our Lady and the biggest day of the year in Knocknagoshel, north Kerry, my mother's home village. Dad and herself had great days at the Pattern Festival, or 'The Pattern,' as it's called. He was full of fun and poems.

Dad won the 100 yards and the long jump. Mary is our mother's first name and she died last Friday, on the fifteenth of August, the feast day of Our Lady's assumption in to heaven.

Mam said you could always rely on Holy Mary. When we were small she would ask Holy Mary to mind us. There was always a candle lighting before exams in front of her statue.

My mother's own mother died when she was four, and the little girl prayed to Holy Mary. There was a day in the kitchen when I found Mam crying behind the closed curtains.

"What's wrong?" I asked. It took a while but Mam, who was never ever sorry for herself, said: "I'm older today than my mother."

Poor Mam, but then within a few minutes she was stocking the shelves in the little pub we ran together and getting on with life in that practical way of hers.

It wasn't easy going in to the pub on Friday. I went in on my own. I should have brought the family. The pub was empty and I never felt so alone. I was taken in to the pub by my parents when I wasn't fit to work for anyone who wasn't family, after a succession of self-inflicted disasters. Mam helped me get my confidence back with a mix of tough love and mother's love. I'm fine and strong now. She knew that before she died. Thanks Mam.

For those of you who are dying or afraid of dying, I sort of feel that death is only the beginning of a journey and not the end. It's not that I'm not heartbroken, because I am. I saw more of Mam than anyone else.

But I'm fairly sure there's something going on after we die. The smile on Mam's face would convince you, and there was the night we were in the Gaiety Theatre in Dublin for the opening of 'The Field,' just before she was diagnosed with the cancer when Dad was with her. Dad isn't gone away.

As we walked in to the theatre, she said: "Look John, a full house." She was talking to Dad. And later she told me she felt his presence beside her, there in his beloved Gaiety.

Mam lived on her own above the pub with Dad's spirit. She tried to retire to "a private house" but came back to the pub after just two days. She missed the street.

"On the first day I saw a dog and on the second day I saw a cat and that was it," she said.

But the real reason was, she knew Dad's spirit was happiest in the home they made over the pub. It was tiny and I often wonder how we all fitted in, but home is where the heart is.

Those last days were tough for sure, but full of love. My brothers, Conor and John, and our sister, Joanna, were never so united. They were so good to Mam. It was like back when we were kids, all sleeping under blankies together on the floor. We always kept in touch but this was us as a family all together with Mam at the end.

I will never forget these days with my brothers and sister. And thanks to the Bons in Tralee. Mam was never in pain.

We said poems for Mam and sang for her as she lay dying. I just got up to hold Mam's hand, right at her last breath. Joanna told Mam what a great mother she was. John made jokes and kept her laughing. Conor, as ever, was the soundest.

Maybe because her own mother died so young, Mam tried so hard to be the best mother ever. It wasn't easy trying to run a pub, never mind four cracked kids and looking after Dad, who needed massive back-up when he was writing all those masterpieces.

Mam was tough, fearless and fiercely independent. So there I was at her bedside, saying: "Mam, you minded us and now we're minding you," feeling so wonderful about myself when Mam said; "I always minded myself. There's no one minding me."

Mam was all for divorce, contraception and gay rights. She was no old-fashioned Irish Mammy who did as she was told. Mam was well able for Dad, but in a good way. She always spoke her mind and was full of wisdom. Our mother's last advice to her grandkids on relationships was: "If there's an argument going on, one of you has to shut up." She defined post-feminism even before feminism.

I'll miss our favourite summer feed of ham, cabbage, cream and the first of the new potatoes. I'll miss her being around the bar. She even threw a lad out just a few months ago. And I'm dreading this evening when we'll be closing the coffin. That's the toughest part.

When I started off writing this, I was all brave and philosophical. The pain of her loss is bad now. But I hear our Mam. "Toughen up," she says.

The maternal-induced composure came back again just now. I'm certain Mam picked her day to meet up with Dad. The day didn't pick her.

Heaven, I think, is here all around us. Mam smiles, and Dad is making up poems for her.

HE DOESN'T MIND MY
TELLING AND I WANT TO
SHOUT MY LOVE OUT FROM
THE ROOFTOPS. I WANT
TO SHOUT MY LOVE IN A
PLACE WHERE ECHOES
LIVE AND REPRODUCE

2

Finally I'm Not Ashamed To Say It: I've Fallen Hopelessly In Love With A Man

January 27, 2014

'M in love with a man. This will come as a shock to those of you who know me well. I have children, four at last count, and just the one wife, but I have fallen hopelessly in love with a man.

Yes, a man. A lovely man. I have known him since I was born, at a very early age. I'd love to give him a big hug. Right now. He's here with me, watching the laptop screen as I type. So why not? Go on, he says. Go on, do it. Hug him to bits. I've done it. Hugged him, that is. Ahhhh but it feels so good.

I have this man's permission to reveal his identity. He doesn't mind my telling and I want to shout my love out from the rooftops. I want to shout my love in a place where echoes live and reproduce. I have rubbed oil on his body. I have put my fingers through his receding hair. I sleep with him every single night. There have been intimacies. Love is all that counts.

Oh, but he's so good to me. Yes, yes, yes, I'm in love with a wonderful man and I don't care a damn what anyone says or thinks.

This is the first time I have come out. I knew all along this was the love I dared not speak. Even those closest to me were not aware of this confession. There's a daughter who reads this every Monday morning. I just cannot understand why it took so long. I should have declared my love years and years ago. I feel as if a lifetime of delights has been wasted but it's never too late. Never too late to fall in love. We are an item now.

Every day I tell him I love him and that I care for him. I forgive him his faults. There's a portrait of him in my bathroom and when I'm shaving I look at him and say: "I love you, man." Well, every morning since I declared my love, which was only the day before yesterday. So if you add it up, tomorrow will be the third anniversary in days.

He was my first love but for many years I rejected him. Told him he wasn't good enough to be loved by me. He was hurt. There is nothing worse than not being loved by those deserving of your love.

You know from the very beginning you should treat him with respect. There's the constant nagging and gnawing away at him and his self-confidence. I was concentrating on his faults. If he did something worthy of acclaim, you just shrug it off and move on, in case he got big-headed. In case he thinks he's better than anyone else. It's an Irish thing, I think. Belittling those you love "for their own good."

So you drag him down. Make him small. Maybe it was because others did not see his qualities and I took their lead rather than make my own judgment. You know how it is. If 10 people tell you good stuff about you and just the one is critical, it's the bad one we remember. Our opinion is formed by a minority of negativity.

Here, in this very public forum, I want to apologise unreservedly for any hurt I may have caused to him. Yes, I was very hard on the man I love when he made mistakes. I would give out to him all night long.

Sometimes I would drive him to drink. More days I would get mad with him and he took it out on others. There were days when he found it hard to get out of bed and face the day. But did I say: "I love you, man. Get up and carry on?" No, I did not.

Why was it I singled him out for the kind of abuse I wouldn't dream of inflicting on another human being? A word of encouragement was all that was needed. Every now and then. I never allowed him forgiveness for past indiscretions. I constantly reminded this poor man of his faults every day.

I know now, in mid-life, I should have loved him from the

beginning. But he still loves me. Deep down. Self-doubt and low self-esteem kept me from accepting the love that was my due.

I will now reveal the name of the man I love for the very first time in public.

His name is me.

Yes, it's good to love yourself. If you don't love yourself, how do you expect others to love you?

So starting today, go easy on you. Be nice to yourself. Pet yourself. Talk to yourself at work in the supportive way you would to a cherished colleague who has made a mistake. You know the way you open the door for people out of politeness? Well open the door for you. For years you have been living next door to Alice. Well you're Alice.

I'm only at this self-love two days and already I feel better. I hope I won't break it off with myself.

So go on, give yourself a big hug. Go on, you good thing. How good is that?

> THE IDEA OF QUEUEING
> UP WITH DISJOINTED
> GREYHOUNDS SUFFERING
> FROM DIARRHOEA AND
> WHINGEING CALVES
> WITH DISLOCATED HIPS
> IN HIS 'SURGERY'
> DIDN'T APPEAL TO ME

| 3 |

You'd Be Surprised What The Touch Of A Toe Can Do

May 22, 2012

L AST Saturday night the lively wedding band were asking for directions to Amarillo. Somewhere between 'sha la-la la-la la la la' and 'and sweet Marie who waits for me,' my voice broke. Then it disappeared into a whisper. I wouldn't be heard singing behind a newspaper now. But there was worse to come.

The back went when we got stuck into Neil Diamond's 'Sweet Caroline'. The stretch for "hands touching hands" went fine but it was the "reaching out" for the red fingernails of the tall girl in the stilts for heels that finished me off. The pain from the spasms is like a having a baby every six minutes.

Mothers of sextuplets deserve every penny of their children's allowance and every free nappy too.

I was warned off dancing but when the band starts playing it's very hard to resist a gallop.

Last week I was filling a pint when down I went, like I was shot by a gun. Jonathan Sexton's dad Jerry was taking some light refreshments at the end of the counter. He rushed in, thinking I had a heart attack.

"I don't know how to do mouth to mouth," he said.

"It's my back that's gone not my heart." Who would be a Samaritan?

The jokes started immediately. One lad said: "Ah Billy, sure you're stiff in all the wrong places now." Hilarious.

Then someone told me I should go see a back fixer but the idea of queueing up with disjointed greyhounds suffering from diarrhoea and whingeing calves with dislocated hips in his 'surgery' didn't appeal to me.

There can be no doubt but that weddings are dangerous occasions.

My beautiful dote of a cousin, Triona, married John Docherty, who is lovely too.

Fr Pat Moore was the priest. He is a writer and the kind of man Jesus had in mind when he was picking apostles. He's a stand-up priest.

Pat's last play was about a man with a pimple on his arse.

"No east Kerry man," preached the priest, "is complete until he marries a north Kerry woman. Now he's finished."

Triona and John are made for each other. In their case one plus one equals one but marriage is the hardest game of all.

My cousin, Pierre, and his wife, Martina, came from South Africa for the big day out. Martina brought two-year-old Clara to meet her Kerry cousins. Martina is Cape Malay and mother and baby were dipped in the perfect colouring for human beings. If some day science allows parents to pick the skin colour of their newborn baby from a catalogue, like they do in the paint shops, my choice would be Cape Malay. It's a sallow shade of subtle, silky, light- brown. Baby Clara has a lovely galaxy of Irish freckles.

I was the best man at their wedding in the wine country of Franschooek, about four years ago. Pierre plays with the Cape Symphony Orchestra and they were his wedding band. The wedding service was held outdoors on a sunny, autumn day in February. As we waited for the bride I asked Pierre what religion he was getting married in?

"Haven't a clue. Might be some kind of Lutheran," he said. And he didn't care either once he put the ring on Martina's finger. They are still very much in love.

Pierre reminded me I started off the best man's speech by asking for all the curtains to be pulled across.

"Now Martina, that's how we do foreplay in Ireland."

Well, they must have learned from the demonstration because Martina is expecting number two.

As a barman I get to hear people's troubles all the time. It only costs €3.90 for a pint and the State gets about 40pc of that back in taxes. We should be funded by the HSE and the VHI.

My totally random, anecdotal research indicates about 40pc of people are happily married.

I'm not really sure exactly why marriage can be such a war zone.

Here's a simplified, rendered analysis. Maybe it's down to payback for the times when women were slaves both in the kitchen and the bedroom.

Women made scones and babies. The men were in charge of everything else.

Those slave wives reared their daughters to be independent and they in turn passed it on to the next generation and now maybe the revolution has gone too far as often happens when great wrongs need to be righted.

When I was a kid I complained to my mother that there were flecks of dirt in the milky, white sliced bread. She explained that when the bakers changed from making brown bread to white, some of the brown flour was still in the machine and it blended into the first batch of white sliced pans. There are always parts of the old processes that linger on. Some men still suffer hangovers from the remains of the days of their ascendancy.

Both sides need to find a middle ground. The merest touch of a conciliatory toe, stretched out across the imaginary but sometimes barbed-wire border under the duvet will solve most problems. But who will make the first move?

**IT ALSO SEEMS MAGPIES
ARE VERY INTELLIGENT. A
MAGPIE MIGHT HAVE THE
PROBLEM-SOLVING SKILLS OF
A SEVEN-YEAR-OLD CHILD**

| 4 |

One For Sorrow, Two For Joy... The Magpie's Life Is In Your Hands

June 15, 2015

THERE are laws to stop dogs barking but nothing can be done to shut up the magpies. How does he keep the raucous call going on for so long?

The magpies' throat must have been wiped with sandpaper basted in acid. I'm cracking up from it. The magpie alarm tone is worse than a nail scraping glass.

The magpie wakes us up about half an hour after dawn, and his horrible calls go on for about three hours. The lyrics are staccato, hoarse and repetitive, like mad English punk bands singing horrible things about the queen.

I'm pretty sure he's squatting in our disused chimney. What am I to do? Send him a solicitor's letter?

I was thinking of going up on a ladder. But guns, heights and birds scare me.

And, yes, a homeowner can legally murder magpies, the logic being the magpies plunder the nests of game birds such as the pheasant. I now have a licence to kill and hold the power of life and death.

I'm counting now. His call goes out in five one-caw verses and there's a delay of about two seconds between each round.

I'm not sure if I could pull the trigger. What if the little baby magpies were there outside the house all day mourning the dead mammy or daddy. They say crows have funerals and the magpie is a cousin of the crow, and all those birds coming round cawing sorry for your troubles could result in some of them getting to like the place. And the problem could be compounded.

I don't know any bird undertakers who would take the corpse to its last resting place.

Maybe I can justify the killing.

I used to go to a chipper in Dublin and they got done for passing pigeons off as chickens. Their fried chicken was never the same afterwards so I check if magpies can be eaten. It seems so, but the taste is horrible. And the magpies eat mice, lizards and oozy roadkill.

There's a fly-tying business in London and the tiers pay £3 per pair of magpie wings.

That's fly-tying as in producing flies for fishing. I'm not sure, though, if I would like to wipe out the whole species and have thousands of dead magpies scattered across the Irish prairies like slaughtered buffalo but if you shot a thousand, well then that's three grand.

So with killing in mind, I contact a shootist.

"I'll get 'em," he says. "They're pretty much sitting ducks."

I laugh at his joke but wonder if it's appropriate.

He went off for a while, the magpie, but he's back and now I want to kill him with my bare hands.

But then I get to thinking.

The Irish Wild Bird Conservancy are of the opinion that man's messing about with habitats causes more damage to small birds than magpies. It also seems magpies are very intelligent. A magpie might have the problem-solving skills of a seven-year-old child.

I'm finding it hard to think with the incessant cawing.

The magpie must die. So I call the shootist again and book him to shoot the magpie but I tell him I will not be present for the cull, which is a nicer word than killing.

Then I do the math. One from two is one and if I have the magpie killed, then that leaves one magpie.

There's an old rhyme about the magpies that goes: "One for sorrow, two for joy."

The magpie widow could bring us terrible luck by way of revenge.

We had a friend in the old days and he was the only one of our crew to own a car. He would turn back the car for home if he spotted a solitary magpie. We had to pretend so see another one and would go: "There he is behind the ditch."

"Where?" our friend would ask.

And our reply was: "He flew off, you've just missed him."

And we managed to get to our destination.

Then there's the stories of magpies collecting gold and silver. Maybe there's a Derrynaflan hoard in the nest.

The screecher mightn't even be male. It's hard to identify which is which. Magpies aren't exactly donkeys.

The thoughts of culling a jeweller with the brain of a seven-year-old bothers me greatly. And there might be chicks on the way.

But just this very second he or she is joined by several more magpies.

Their harmonies aren't exactly Simon and Garfunkel and, like bad trad, every tune sounds the same.

What's left of my mind isn't fully made up, so what say you? Yae or nae? I'm taking the Herod option here. Thumbs up or thumbs down?

The magpies' life is in your hands.

THERE WAS NO SHOWING OFF, JUST TEACHING AND SHARING. THE SOFT, GENTLE BUT PASSIONATE VOICE, HOARSE FROM TOO MUCH TALK, IS GONE FOR GOOD NOW

| 5 |

Silver Screen Legend Kieran Helped Us To Dream In Listowel

May 5, 2014

KIERAN GLEESON'S eyes lit up as he explained the background to the film he was showing, and you could see he was excited – excited about sharing all he knew with his audience there in his three-screen cinema in a small country town.

There was always an introduction before his cinema club films on a Thursday night. This was his night, the night when he got to choose the films he loved. Kieran spoke as all the knowledgeable do – in simple, easy-to-understand language.

Kieran has been in love with the cinema ever since he stood up on the piled-high metal boxes that were used for storing magic reels. There, he was the spellbound kid looking out through the porthole in the projectionist's room with his dad and grandad in their country cinema in Cappamore, County Limerick. Afterwards, he would be full of excitement and full of talk.

Kieran 'the man' is still 'the boy' in the projection room. Often, we would be kept on after the crowd had gone home for a discussion about the movie he was showing. He knew his stuff, did Kieran. There was no showing off, just teaching and sharing. The soft, gentle but passionate voice, hoarse from too much talk, is gone for good now.

Kieran's life is a silent movie. He breathes with the help of a machine. Our small town hero's chest rises and falls with every breath. It's as if he's a marathon runner at the end of a gruelling race. Kieran Gleeson – who rescued, owns and loves our local cinema here in Listowel – has advanced Motor Neurone Disease.

But he's still communicating. Kieran writes a little, but only with great effort. He sends text messages, nods in agreement or moves his eyes towards something he wants you to read.

Kieran writes '29' on a sheet of paper and hands it to his wife, Teresa. Did you ever notice it when two people feel and read each other's thoughts? They seem to instinctively know what the other person is thinking. The bond has to be strong, but there's more than just tuning in. The two must share the dream.

The 29 refers to January 29, 1987 – the day the cinema in Listowel reopened under Kieran's management.

The cinema had been closed for two years. Kieran was driving by one day with his mother and he noticed a 'For Sale' sign up over The Astor Cinema. There and then, he made up his mind to buy the rat-infested wreck. A local businessman told Kieran he was "absolutely mad" – and maybe he was. Small town cinemas were going the way of small shops. There are only a few independent cinemas left in Ireland. The prophecy of failure made Kieran all the more determined to succeed. He worked day and night and, bit by bit, the cinema began to pay for itself. His mother helped out every Sunday when the cinema was at its busiest.

Kieran opened three screens and he had the best of films showing at the same time as the big cities. He was one of the first to embrace digitalisation and encouraged Jimmy Deenihan, the then Arts Minister, to provide grant assistance to a number of cinemas.

Hard-up parents were given deals. Kids who didn't have enough money were never refused. Kieran often declined the big money-making movies if he felt they were bad. He never overcharged for tickets, sweets or popcorn. Director Ger Barrett – who is now about to release his third movie, 'Brain on Fire', later this year – was allowed in for free.

Ger premiered his last movie, 'Glassland', in Listowel – and the night was turned into a tribute to his mentor and friend. Actor Jack Reynor came along and Kieran was so buzzed up that the illness was put into remission for a night. It was like the football coach who sees the player he trained as a kid step up to collect an All-Ireland medal.

I was only three, but I remember being brought to The Astor for 'Summer Holiday' by Bernie Buckley – who was babysitting me then, and still does. Dad and I cried when Davy Crockett died at the Alamo. It was here I had the first lip-kiss in the back seat.

Sometimes, when our kids were young, we'd be there at the pictures and, out of the corner of my eye, I could see Kieran standing in the aisle at the back, taking it all in. He was enjoying the kids enjoying the picture show. The light flickered over his smiling face and, if ever there was man who was happy at work, well, it was him. There and then, and always. After all, he gave up his studies in accountancy to help run the family cinema in Cappaghmore when his dad died suddenly from a heart attack.

There have been tough times and, last year, thousands of euro were stolen from the safe by heartless thieves. Teresa is trying to get to grips with the details of running a cinema, but she's learning fast. Best of all, she and Kieran are determined to keep the cinema going. "Our staff have been so good to us," she says.

Kieran had been checking out the possibility of live streaming concerts and sporting events. He had big plans.

The kids come in from school and Kieran gets a smile out. Teresa, I know, struggles to come to terms with how it is that such a decent man suffers so much. She is loyal to him as a full-time carer on a break from her job in the civil service, and loyal to his vision for the family-run cinema. Such is the practicality of true love and mutual respect.

Teresa sent me a link to a Radio Kerry interview with John Herlihy, where Kieran speaks of his love of the sounds of the old cinema projection room with the 35mm reels. "We treasure that now," she says. "It's all we have of his voice."

He shuffles in his wheelchair to attract my attention. He shows me the screen on his phone. This week, Kieran is showing 'The

Revenant' and 'Creed', as well as kids' movies. Still promoting his cinema as he fights for every movement. There is such a powerful, undefeated will within him. As I leave, I kiss my friend gently on the head and thank him for all he has done for all of us.

| 6 |

Who Needs A Man When You've Got Your Pension Book?

May 19, 2014

I DIDN'T need anything but I still went to the shop in the hope of meeting the woman who hasn't had sex for 37 years. She was a no show. I'd have stayed longer but the rain was drizzling down in an annoying way. Annoying like those little mini ribs of hair that stick to the collar of your shirt after a trip to the barber.

I'll bet you feel itchy just thinking about it.

The worst ones are the sneaky, tiny clipped ribs that somehow find their way to the middle of your back. How they get there is a complete friggin' mystery. The hairdresser puts a towel around your neck and your clothes are tight enough but the little rogue mini rib still makes its way to the part of your back you can't quite reach.

I'm getting very bad now from thinking about the itch. Maybe I have fleas. Or are fleas extinct, victims of pesticides like DDT?

When I was a boy all the mothers used to shovel DDT under the under sheet, or the last sheet or whatever it was called.

The fleas were wiped out but subsequent studies have shown what's bad for fleas is bad for humans. I'm not sure if the DDT killed as many humans as fleas but for sure it can't have been good for us. The mothers used to think they were bad mothers if they didn't spread the DDT, such was the power of advertising.

The rogue mini-hairs are a bit like that survivor sperm who makes it all the way. He's a hardy buck, that lone sperm, the Marco Polo of procreation, yet he is an unsung hero.

I was hoping to meet the woman who hasn't had sex for 37 years because she always has deadly mad opinions for columns. She comes out with some great statements as well.

I asked her if she'd like to marry again. The last husband died on her and it wasn't as long as 37 years ago either. I'd say it was the frustration got him in the end. I'd also say women don't realise how important sex is for men. Sorry, that should read some women.

There are many who are most obliging and considerate, even when they are not in the best of form.

I'm not sure if the woman who hasn't had sex for 37 years would even like some. She doesn't even buy the women's mags that are always on about experimental sex.

Thirty Seven, as I call her, gets 'Ireland's Own', which is also easily my favourite magazine. There's no sex in it but there's lots of really interesting articles about history, nature, phenomena and believe it or nots.

So when I asked 37 why she would never again get married, she replied: "I wouldn't swap my Con Houlihan for any man."

Up to the time when she only hadn't had the sex for about 34 years, I used to think that her going on about it was some kind of plaintive cry for attention, or even a broad hint.

But looking back on it now, it may have been that I was thinking like a man. I'm now coming to the opinion that she's on an abstinence protest. Her late husband was a serial philanderer.

Few, if any people in Listowel know her identity.

So much so that some sceptics doubt if she actually exists but she does and sad to say there are thousands more like her all over the country and beyond.

Possibly, the reason Missus 37 told me her shocking story was that she knew I would put it in the paper. But Missus never buys the paper because she says "there's nothing in it."

It could still be a protest, though, in that she only told me, and me alone, of her secret about not having the sex for the 37 years.

I'm pretty sure of that much. So if she only tells me, the only writer she knows, and the only writer she knows who is as cracked as herself, it could be that she is trying to make a statement and that I am her messenger. I feel used. I'm not in favour of people not having sex for 37 years. It's bad for men and for women.

Just a word of warning for the neighbours which arises from an encounter with a woman who wrongly guessed the identity of Missus 37.

I dearly love Listowel but our gossips get their facts wrong more often than even newspaper reporters.

Here's the warning. If you see me talking to a woman who is old enough not to have had sex for 37 years, please do not assume she is the one, because you would be wrong. I know I'm wasting my time. When do the facts ever get in the way of a good gossip?

It could be that Missus 37 has come to the conclusion that all men are idiots. She might be right. Last week we told you of how the mother received a marriage proposal in the post, accompanied by a bar of nutty chocolate.

This week he sent her a party pack consisting of a bar of Turkish Delight, a holy picture of Saint Theresa of Avila and a scratch card. This is a sinister development. Turkish Delight is the mother's favourite chocolate.

She refused to eat it, but I did and I won a fiver from the scratching.

KIRBY CALLED HIM YOUNG MOORE'S ALMANAC. MOORE WAS INQUISITIVE AND LEARNED QUICKLY. WHEN WE WERE RAISING A HULLABALOO, HE WAS READING DICKENS UNDER THE DESK

Moore, The Man Who Finds The Soul In All Of Us

Mar 16, 2015

'W HERE'S Moore?" asked one of the lads. "Gone off to be a priest," replied Sullivan. I got a fit of laughing. "Moore a priest? Sure he's mad for the girls."

It was September and we were in third year in St Michael's College in Listowel. We all called each other by our surnames. I was Kane, the 'e' was dropped, and Moore was Moore.

Kirby called him Young Moore's Almanac. Moore was inquisitive and learned quickly. When we were raising a hullabaloo, he was reading Dickens under the desk. Moore was always in trouble, though. For telling jokes and sitting near me. He was one of the lads but more refined and gentle than the rest of us.

I missed him. Moore used to calm the cracked me. By just being Moore. He was funny but serene too. A Buddha in a boy's body. I can't remember a single word he said but I do recall the way he made us feel. Moore, even then, knew that there was more going on.

It was Sunday Mass in St Brigid's Church in Duagh. Standing room only. There was lively flute music and a sermon about calling to see contrary people. "Deep down," said the priest, "they were looking for love, like the rest of us, and if you persisted at the very worst you would get a good winner at the races in Listowel for the good deed." Laughter in church.

The priest was tired-looking. He works all hours. His mother died a few months back. The priest believes in the hereafter, but he misses her so much.

He is the driving force behind the new community centre and the live crib with a real cow and a real donkey. The priest lives in one room in the big old presbytery. The front door is never locked and the people of the parish can meet whenever they like in the sitting rooms. The kitchen is part of the open house.

Then just before the Mass was over, Moore told a joke. Laughter filled up the church. On the way out, we were greeted by the chimes of 'Danny Boy' from the electronic church bell. For the emigrants who had left Duagh. To remember them and to remind people to work hard to keep the village alive.

My old school friend is Fr Pat now. He is so loved here in Duagh. He has this way of bringing out the best in us. Moore treats us all the same. He exists on many different levels. From the philosophical to the funny. But it's all underpinned by love and a spirituality that brings heaven to the here and now.

Three weeks ago Moore was diagnosed with cancer of the oesophagus.

"Is it true, Pat?"

"Yes, but we will deal with it. How's your mother?"

I gulped. Choked back the tears. We met and he read me, as he does. "It's all good, the tumour hasn't spread. They'll bombard it and we'll see then." We hugged. Moore and me. I could see the boy in him when we talked about a trip to Rome.

Moore wrote about his cancer in the Duagh parish magazine.

"I mindfully think of the tumour that I saw so clearly in the PET scan and I engage with it. What information is it bringing? What is it saying? What emotional and shadowy stuff is it bringing up? Then to sit in the presence of an icon, the Eucharist, a sacred memory and allow the Divine light into me through that, going to my head, my throat, my heart and my gut."

He didn't say too much about the prognosis to me or anyone else.

I wonder what it's like for Moore when he's alone in the dark of the night. Does he worry? Is he afraid?

Moore, being Moore, will embrace the cancer. The reason being that he will learn more about the greater scheme. And he will bring the fellow cancer patients along with him. Right now he's trying to answer the questions, like why me? And what's next?

It's not so much what he says, but it's that too. Moore writes brilliantly. It's more his easy ways and gentle manner that send a message that calm is the way to go through life. And he is holy. Very holy. But not a saint. Unless your definition of a saint is someone who has human frailties and puts others before himself. He loves women's company and drinking endless cups of tea and he's mad for the road.

Moore is a man. One of us.

It's not that my pal craves publicity but more like that by getting his story told, or telling it himself in the online parish newsletter, that he is simply doing his job of preaching and bringing Jesus in to all our lives.

Please say a prayer for my friend Moore.

He'd love that.

SCHILLACI WAS THE LEAST MATERIALISTIC MAN I KNEW. A MINIMALIST. HIS PLEASURE WAS IN GIVING, USUALLY TO BOOKIES AND PUBLICANS

| 8 |

Our Schillaci Was A Man Of Little Vices But No Sins

October 22, 2011

PAT O'DONOGHUE fell off a stool in John B's on the night Schillaci scored against us at Italia '90. My brother John put the name Schillaci on swarthy Pat and it stuck.

We adopted Schillaci, more or less. He had the freedom of John B's unless he was barred or fired for intoxication or insubordination or both but the banishment only ever lasted a day. For Schillaci was a lovable man, who hadn't an ounce of bad in him.

My dad never barred Schillaci. They looked after each other when they were on the run. Years ago the Mayor of Boston came a calling. John B hid out upstairs. Schillaci was intercepted by the Mayor.

'Do you know the whereabouts of John B Keane?' asked the great man.

'F**k off boy,' was the reply. And off he flew.

Schillaci was a bird who perched here and there and he was always in a fierce hurry even when he was going nowhere. There was a reason.The poor fella was taken into care when he was a small boy. Only it wasn't care. The Brothers beat him and the verbal torture was even worse.

But he was never bitter. It was as if he accepted his lot. Like it was normal to suffer. But he was a happy man most of the time.

Schillaci was mad about kids and he loved to read to his own grandchildren. I suppose it was his way of reclaiming his lost childhood.

Money burned a hole in his pocket. He drew his social on a Wednesday and wasn't he the independent man. Tim O'Carroll, his friend, used to call it state sponsored terrorism. But the bounty seldom lasted longer than Saturday.

When Schillaci was moving into his flat a few years ago he owned only two spoons. I tipped off my mother. "Have you cutlery?" she asked.

"Sure the house is full of it," he replied.

Schillaci was the least materialistic man I knew. A minimalist. His pleasure was in giving. Usually to bookies and publicans but when he got the compo for his mistreatment from the Brothers Grim he redistributed his wealth among the less fortunate around the town and bought presents for everyone.

Listowel took him into care and in return he looked after all of us. Schillaci had the run of 30 houses. The women loved his company and he was welcome for dinner any time without prior notice or even a knock on the door. But he was a gourmet and a literary critic. The Brothers did teach him how to read and that was how our bird found his freedom. He was a three book a week man.

"How did you get on in X's house?" we asked.

"Chicklit and curry," he replied in disgust.

Schillaci was badly cut when he fell the night after he scratched Ballabrigs the winner of the Aintree Grand National from his betting slip.

"What happened?"

"Inspectin' roads boy."

He was, without doubt, the most unsuccessful punter I have ever met. There were more losers last Saturday week. Pat Schillaci called in to John B's for the last time. He borrowed three euro.

"Hey b'y," he said, "that's the kind of reckless lendin' that has the country where it is."

The man was totally honest. He would always pay you back. By cleaning a window (in patches) or cutting a lawn (in tufts) or minding the kids or by giving you a good laugh. After my dad died he invited himself to Sunday lunch with my mother. Schillaci sensed when you were down and he never ever judged.

My mother who ruled Schillaci with tough love was taking a fiver a week off him for Christmas. So he could stand to his grandkids.

When he missed a payment we were worried. His neighbour Michael let me into the flat. Schillaci was on the floor, half-way to the door. He died of a massive tumour. The doctors say he didn't suffer.

Our town is far from perfect. No place is, but we gave the little bird from Cobh a fitting send off. Mary Brophy organised it all. Mick McConnell sang 'The Parting Glass.' The choir sang their hearts out. Fr Ashe said a lovely mass and the church was full. I gave the final oration for my pal.

He will be missed by his sons and grandkids but most of all by Mary, his wife. They split up years ago and were getting back together in a few weeks. Schillaci told my wife Elaine only a few days before he died: "I will always love Mary."

Thanks to the emergency services for their professionalism and for the respect they gave to our friend in extremis. I was on my own with Schillaci in his flat while Michael went to the door of the building to watch out for the ambulance.

There was blood, I panicked. The calm emergency nurse was on the phone and asked if I could hear breathing. I put my head on Schillaci chest and moved my ear near to his mouth. Not a sound. I had never seen the scrawny bird so still. That was the hardest part.

There was a crumpled betting docket lying on the couch. I opened it out. '2e Ireland@ 33/1 to win the World Cup.'

Now we know why we lost. I was about to whisper an Act of Contrition to Schillaci when I thought, "hey Billy boy, hold on here a minute."

Sure that man had no sins.

MAYBE SOMEWHERE DEEP INSIDE MY SMALL BOY'S HEAD I KNEW I WOULD BE A SWALLOW SOME DAY AND WOULD TAKE LONG AND STORMY JOURNEYS

A Song For Our Swallows, Who Will Always Find Their Way Back Home

September 22, 2014

WHEN the kids were young we used to welcome the swallows home to our old turfshed with a song. It went: "Welcome to the swallows, welcome to Co Kerry, welcome to the swallows, welcome for a cup of tea."

The last line evolved into "welcome to make your pee." The pee song was repeated every time a swallow flew by. Kids love bold words and the swallows dipped their wings like planes at an air show by way of thanking the children for their tribute.

When I was a small boy, I prayed for the little birds every night.

We had old stores out the back of the pub and the swallows nested in holes in the stone walls or in the joins under beams and lintels.

Maybe somewhere deep inside my small boy's head I knew I would be a swallow some day and would take long and stormy journeys. I had a lovely upbringing but when I was a small boy I was a secret worrier.

The swallows are fine and fat now after this lovely summer.

Scatters gather in high-wire conclave as they discuss the departure date of their winter holidays.

The weather is changing this week and the colder climate kills off the insects.

Small birds can be sent hundreds and even thousands of miles off course by a bad storm. The heroes will be exhausted and broken, their tiny food reserves rapidly depleting, like a plane running out of fuel, but on they fly for home.

How is it, then, that they can find their way back home to a hay shed in a place where even the postman gets lost?

The swallows' message to their babies is: "You must always have a plan to come home because it is the coming home that keeps the clan from extinction."

When the youngsters told us they were on their way to America or Australia because there was no work here I'd always say: "Make a plan, make a plan to come home. We need ye to come back to keep our place alive with new ideas and new energy."

The swallows lost their homes in the so-called boom. Old places where generation after generation nested were knocked away.

Seven or eight years ago, I put in a cold room, out at the back of the pub. It was January and I forgot about the swallows.

They came back in the summer but the right of way to the nest under the roof leading to the back door had two big fans whirring and buzzing day and night.

The disappointed swallows flew in and out several times, wondering what had happened to their ancestral home.

I felt as if I was a lender who had repossessed a family dwelling.

I'm not sure where they were relocated, but the swallows are resilient and phlegmatic.

The late spring of 2013 started off fine and warm. Then the cold and the rains came.

The insects didn't hatch and the little birds died in their thousands. There were never so few arrivals as in April and May of this year.

Niall Hatch of Birdwatch Ireland tells me, though, that this warm, dry summer was a good one for swallows.

They are all born here in Ireland. The swallows migrate for feeding, not breeding.

The mother lays an egg a day and when she has seven or eight, she will hatch them out.

The gestation period is only a few weeks and the mother can give birth to as many as four broods in the one year.

There was this old boy who used to drink in the pub and he would point to his big beer belly and say: "It cost a lot of money to put that there."

The darting swallows feed in flight all summer long.

Now their efforts have paid off. Every swallow's belly is full and it cost to put it there.

The swallows fly more slowly now as they try to conserve energy for the long journey ahead.

Soon they will gather in groups in out-of-the-way places or on electricity wires in the towns and cities.

Our heroes have to cross over an ocean, several seas, the Pyrenees, the Atlas Mountains, the Sahara Desert and the length of Africa before they find their home places.

The small boy and girl run in to the kitchen with their news. The kids start to sing: "Welcome to the swallows, welcome to South Africa".

OLLIE IS MAKING THE MOST OUT OF THE VISIT TO HIS BAR BY PRESIDENT OBAMA. THERE'S A NICE CROWD IN THE PUB, AND MOST – UNLIKE THE VIKINGS – ARE SPENDING MONEY

| 10 |

Moneygall Is The Village That Found A President – I Just Hope It Never Loses Its Charm And Soul

July 9, 2012

THERE were green and black wellingtons hanging from hooks like sleeping bats. Biscuits and socks cosied up beside tins of pears and beans. Homemade jams and breads were matched up on the counter. And a cream guaranteed to cure mastitis. Harrods hasn't such a choice.

It's a small country store. Friendly chat is part of the buying. Better by far than dealing with some listless superstore automaton of a young one, who only ever smiles at closing time on pay day.

"I don't know much about sheep myself," John Donovan, the owner, explains, "but it seems the lambs go swingin' the tails when they're dungin'. The rings take the tail off. For hygiene reasons."

It seems the fluffy tail attracts dung. The dung attracts bluebottles and greenbottles. They lay eggs that turn into maggots.

John also does a nice line in Obama souvenirs. Rulers, key rings and fridge magnets. That sort of thing. John owns the president's ancestral home and I bought a few bits for my friend, Paul Manning, who had the maddest and best birthday party ever this weekend. Paul has MS and if ever a man epitomised 'Is feidir linn', it's young Manning.

"It might be the last time I'll play the guitar in Listowel," he tells us. The fingers are beginning to seize up and as he swung his wheelchair round the party, inside we were crying, but we rejoiced too. Eighty or more singers and musicians played their very hearts out for Paul. And he rose to the occasion and sang and played us all into a frenzy.

I was tempted to buy Paul a pot of 'Muddy Marvel De-Scab' from John's store. Paul can't hold a plectrum anymore and his fingers are raw from the strumming.

It's the kind of shop you just don't leave before John finds out everything. But that's not down to nosiness. It's more that he is genuinely interested in people. So much so, he looks after his customers from the cradle to the grave. John is also the local funeral director. He's such an enterprising man you'd nearly die just to give him the bit of business.

It's the weekend of the American Festival in Moneygall. The Stars and Stripes flutter in the gentle breeze as the excited swallows, well recovered now from their jet lag, fly madly in every direction.

A bus pulls in outside Ollie Hayes's pub. The tourists are from somewhere in Scandinavia. The visitors go to the toilet and take pictures beside the cardboard cut-out of Barack Obama, but not one of the miserable bastards buys a drink.

Ollie wasn't in but we go back a bit. He was a bishop when he met his wife. A bishop in 'The Field', and the lovely Majella was the publican's wife in the play. She's a publican's wife in real life now – and very good at it too.

Ollie is making the most out of the visit to his bar by President Obama. There's a nice crowd in the pub, and most – unlike the Vikings – are spending money.

There's Obama cupcakes and T-shirts with 'What's the craic, Barack?' written on the front.

A widescreen TV shows the visit on a continuous loop.

The pool room is now an art gallery. The pool table is draped with a white tablecloth as part of an exhibition. Is it an 37 yearslation? Or maybe it's just a pool table draped with a white tablecloth.

The bar walls are covered with Obama memorabilia, flanked

on either wing by pictures of Tipp hurling teams. Behind the bar is the glass the president drank from, and the 50 he left for the drink is on public display.

Michelle, the bar person, is a student. She has a lovely smile and winning ways. The bar employs a good few locals.

This lad lounging outside the door told me if I ever wanted a green card all I had to do was ask Ollie as Ollie had Barack's mobile and they were never off the phone to each other and they were always going on the lash together in America and Barack as much as gave Ollie the keys of Air Force One.

To us barmen the rings on a pint glass are as sure a measure of ageing as the rings on an oak tree.

This glass lasted him a while, I'd say. He was broke. Someone bought him a pint. The green card is in the post.

You'd be lonesome leaving Ollie's. It's a homely place to break the journey and only a minute off the motorway.

Julia Hayes and her husband Joe, who is Ollie's uncle, run the only other pub in the village. It closes by day and so we went round the back through an archway with bedrooms overhead. The backyard is a gem with yellow roses plumper than any you'd find in Texas. The multicoloured flower beds surely came from Babylon and the lawn is so well manicured it must have been cut by a nail scissors.

Julia is 81 and Joe, her husband, a year older. "We lost our partners," said Julia, "and we'll be married 25 years this coming week."

Their pub is cosy and is an extension of the kitchen. It is effectively their living room. Julia is a very open lady, without a wrinkle on her lovely fresh face. Her first husband died young and she lost her only daughter to cancer, "but I have two fine grandchildren". She's sad for a minute as we drink tea and talk about trade and farming.

Joe's son, Kevin, brandishes a fly-squatter. The kitchen is old-fashioned, in the best sort of way, with a big table in the middle and a roasting hot Jubilee range. It's a spotless open house – and fly-free.

Kevin goes out to the garden and brings in rhubarb.

The green and red rhubarb sticks are long, strong and thick. I'd say Kevin had to hack the stalks off the root with a machete.

"For your mother," says Julia.

And how is Henry Hayes I ask? Henry is Obama's cousin and Joe's grand-nephew. He's the man who brought Barack to Moneygall. Ask not what your village can do for you but what you can do for your village.

"Henry is the nicest fella you ever met," says Julia. But Obama never got to Julia and Joe's. "Maybe next time," she says. You could sense her disappointment and she switched the subject by telling us Joe did all the cooking.

There was a kiss goodbye and an invitation to call again.

Later in the day, we heard Henry lost his job. Another victim of this cursed depression.

New tourism can change people and places and, as I drove home, I made a wish for Moneygall: that it might never turn from the truly hospitable village that it is and always has been.

11

Alcohol Reports Won't Tell You Of A Generation Dying Before Our Eyes

April 29, 2013

THE doctors from The Royal College of Physicians in Ireland are asking the government to ban the sponsorship of sporting events by alcohol companies.

Ah yes, lads, and that will be the end of all our troubles. "Oh my goodness," the alcoholic wife-beater will say and "golly" too . "That's it," he will declare. "Now that the Heineken Cup is to be called the Ice Cream trophy, I'm not going to drink another drop."

The young girl who has downed her eighth shot in a heaving club looks up at the poster of the Guinness All-Ireland Hurling Championship and she tells her friends: "I'm switching to Guinness cos I love the small ball."

The report does not say where the replacement sponsorship monies will come from, or how the woman who keeps guests for the Guinness-sponsored Listowel Races will pay for the college registration fees, or who will compensate her son for losing his job as a gateman at the racetrack and collecting glasses in the local pub that night.

There is no mention in the report of the investment of the millions of sponsorship in sporting facilities and coaching by the sporting organisations or as to how these millions will be found if the drinks companies are forced to pull out.

I do not want in any way to belittle the compilers of the report who have risen to the top of their profession by hard work and the excellence of their performance in the field. Sporting events bring the crowds. There's a socio-economic dimension that will not appear on any chart. Bald figures do not give the overall story and so a section of an otherwise excellent report is deeply flawed.

Sporting events are sponsored by drinks companies and in return the drinks companies get an exclusive on the sale of their products at the racetrack. The sponsorship has little if any bearing on the amount consumed, all it does is decide the product that is being supped.

There is no doubt but that in a perfect world we wouldn't need drink or alcohol company sponsorship; but if the ban comes in, the social wreckage will be nowhere to be seen in the bare statistics. Emigration will get even worse and businesses will close. Our town will be on its knees if Listowel Races cannot find a sponsor to replace Diageo.

The report tells us of the terrible damage being done to our young people from drinking too much. The physicians report a 247pc increase in chronic liver disease among 15- to 34-year-olds. We are told of heart problems and suicide. Young people's lives are ruined before they rightly get going.

The college has done us all a great service. No one can doubt the accuracy of the research. There are times like this when I feel like putting a 'For Sale' sign up on the front window. You worry if you're no worse than the drug pushers. But then I get to thinking.

We have been running our family pub for nearly 60 years and our job is to make life more bearable. I'm always slow to write this because you never know when you will make an absolute mess out of a night in the bar and accidentally serve a drunk who will cause mayhem. Sometimes they can put on a front and fool you. But we try to mind our customers. Many is the man and woman who have been saved from alcoholism and self-harm by a long talk, late at night. There are thousands more like us.

In my opinion, there is a direct correlation between the decline of the traditional pub and the increase in medical fallout from excess drinking. The report acknowledges the part the pub plays in our socialising as opposed to buying drink in garages and the like for home consumption. The decent publican will look after his customers.

There are social constraints. You will not let yourself down by falling down drunk in front of the neighbours. The young lad ordering large vodkas will be taken aside and told: "Stay away from the top shelf." But the pub is struggling and The College of Physicians will be a lot busier when we are gone.

Drink is so ingrained in our culture, we have to play the hand we are dealt. Maybe we shouldn't tell our kids not to drink but rather how to drink and where to drink. This is the best solution I can come up with.

The recommendations in the report are accurate for the most part. Drink in the supermarkets is too cheap. You can buy wine for 60 cent a unit. One of the main reasons for drinking at home is the pubs are too dear.

It used to be house parties were boring, unless it was a wake where the bereaved rowed over their share of the deceased's estate. Most of my generation would never drink at home. It was always taboo. Bad example to the kids and all that. We couldn't wait to escape from domesticity but now all the teens stay indoors. Here's a stat you will not find in any report, but it's true: by my reckoning, about 80pc of 18- to 21-year-olds buy one or fewer drinks in nightclubs or bars.

The damage has been done behind closed doors, long before the victims hit the streets. Ask the gardai. The saddest part is that hardly any of the youngsters will read the Royal College Report. A generation are dying before our very eyes and they don't even know why.

**ON THE MORNING OF THE
FUNERAL THE HIGH TIDE WAS
FROTHING AND VICIOUS.
A HUGE GREY SEAL WAS
WASHED UP ON THE SLIP ROAD
JUST ABOVE THE BEACH**

12

Hard To Believe That Just Five Months Ago The Very Same Sea Licked Our Toes

January 9, 2014

THE heroic men on the Kerry County Council pumps barely saved Ballylongford. The tidy, proud village is about a mile in from the fastest flow of the River Shannon.

On Sunday, a mad unforeseen tide surged up the inlet at a relentless, unstoppable pace and right into the heart of the village. Then 22 homes suffered varying degrees of damage from the surging waters. And 22 families are without flood insurance after another disaster ruined their homes 10 years ago.

The neighbours huddle in little groups outside Ballylongford Church at the funeral of John Francie Ahern from Beale. John Francie was in his 80s and was a feisty, humorous character who loved to tell stories.

His nephew, Paddy McElligott, is building a house right by the water's edge on the Women's Beach of Ballybunion, directly in the line of the tide.

Earlier that morning, the waves crashed into Paddy's house. It was hard to believe that just five months ago the same sea licked our toes like a puppy in the sunniest summer in years.

On the morning of the funeral the high tide was frothing and vicious. A huge grey seal was washed up on the slip road just above the beach. Two seats were ripped up from the cement and vandalised by the confluence of the Shannon and the Atlantic.

The steel doors of Ballybunion Sea and Cliff Rescue's headquarters were smashed open by the waves. A deep sinkhole appeared on the road down to the Men's Beach. Locals say their giant footballing hero 'The Bomber' Liston would barely be seen if he fell in.

Ballybunion Sea and Cliff Rescue were out in all weathers making sure bystanders didn't venture too close to the mountainous seas.

A single car has been parked all week in the lower car park at the golf club. Just a few days before the Big Wind, the Sea Rescuers helped retrieve the owner from the sea.

We commiserated with Paddy McElligott at the back of Ballylongford Church. He told us then the story of his new house on the Women's Beach.

The front door is only 20 steps from the sands. The army bomb disposal unit were on their way to his and wife Mary's beach house, he said.

But Paddy was staying put, out of respect to his uncle. Paddy was told two grenade or rocket launchers were washed up on his site.

Paddy is a man not given to undue panic. He is what you might call phlegmatic. "We'll have to wait and see what happens. I wouldn't know much about bombs anyway," he said. In the meantime, Paddy would help lay his Uncle John Francie to rest.

Some things are more important than houses. And anyway, if the place is blown up, they will hear the explosion from the graveyard down the coast, if the baying wind stills for long enough.

The Tarbert Race – the powerful flow of water running up the middle of the Shannon – is turbulent even on days when the Big River is as calm as a holy water font. It is a river within a river. Local mariner, Micheal Finucane Senior, explains the dangers: "The race carries the entire pressure of the Shannon floods from the north as far up as Cavan, all the way down to the estuary," he said.

"Then when the winds and tide come in together from the North Atlantic, the waves are huge and dangerous. The water rushes up towards Bally and there's no stopping it."

The low pressure sends the floods heading for the village. Local councillor Liam Purtill, my Dad's first cousin, is hoping for compensation for the 22 who have no insurance.

He is fighting hard for Bally. I wonder if their homes were on the banks of the Dodder would money and flood defences be easier to come by?

Paddy McElligott and his wife Mary get good news after the funeral. There were no grenade launchers in his new house. No rocket or Exocet blew up Ballybunion. The Sea Rescue people used old watertight army boxes for storing equipment.

The weapons' boxes were thieved by the tide and washed into Paddy's site. "All the hoo-ha was for nothing," said Paddy, as calm as could be. "It all worked out fine in the end."

It would have taken Uncle John Francie the drinking of three halves of whiskey to tell this one. And then he might tell it again.

It's 8pm in Ballylongford on Monday night. High-tide time. The pump men from Kerry County Council are on standby. Sandbags buttress Novenas.

The tide flows in at about the four-metre level. The village is safe, for now, but even bigger tides are forecast for February and March. If the wind is strong and the Tarbert Race is bubble, bubble, toil and trouble, God only knows what will happen. But for tonight at least, the Estuary girls can celebrate Women's Christmas.

This Women's Christmas night is the anniversary of the Big Wind, when hundreds were killed in 1839. Nature never goes away or gives way. The two Ballys know this. These Ballylongford people love where they live and will not be sent packing by storms or floods.

Cromwell's murderers slaughtered their monks. The O'Rahilly who was killed when he charged the British machine-guns at the Easter Rising came from here. His old home was flooded too. There was fire too. The Black and Tans burned out the village but Bally was rebuilt. Brendan Kennelly, from The Crooked Cross in Ballylongford, sums it up in his poem 'Begin'.

"Though we live in a world that dreams of ending, that always seems about to give in, something that will not acknowledge conclusion, insists that we forever begin."

| 13 |

Woe Is Me, I'm Sick – In The Run-up To Seven Days Of The Best Fun Ever

September 9, 2013

THEY took out my tonsils a long, long time ago. But one grew back. I'll bet if the doctors cut off my leg it wouldn't have grown back. Only sore things grow back.

Now the tonsil on the left is swollen to the size of a turnip. The one on the right is fine. It's dormant. My theory is there were two surgeons. One was vastly experienced and he did the right tonsil. The other surgeon was a trainee. "Go on," says the old doctor, "you have a go at the left one. For the bit of practice."

"Oh feckit," exclaims the young butcher, "but I think I've left a bit of a stump."

"Don't worry in the slightest," comforts the senior man. "By the time that tonsil grows back, I'll be well dead and gone."

This lad I meet in the betting shop says I should claim. He has "whiplash in the back" after getting knocked off his bike and he told me there was collateral damage.

"The libido is fierce low," he says. In a sad voice.

How this could happen after falling off a bike is well beyond me. There are peletons of lycra men peddling like mad on tax-free bikes on every road now. It's very bad for the sex life. If the man in the betting shop is to be believed.

I tell him there might be a slight difficulty with the Statute of Limitations. The tonsil operation took place in 1968.

The throat is as raw as if it had been got at by a cheese grater. Like I've been gargling with sulphuric acid. I can't speak. Not a word. Which some say might not be such a bad thing.

There's another man who gives out free advice and he's a misogynist. He traps me in the bar. Every time I see him coming I feel like putting a 'FOR SALE' sign on the front window.

His theory is women kill thousands of men every year by telling them there's nothing wrong with them.

The misogynist makes out that women are really pissed off with men for not having babies and going through all that pain and carrying around and feeding another person for nine months and losing their figures and getting stretch marks and loads more.

So when a man gets a really sore throat, the ailment is passed off by his partner as an offshoot of man-flu. The man doesn't go the doctor. Six months later, the man dies. Or so the misogynist's theory goes.

I might be wronging the junior doctor who might have operated on the left tonsil back in 1968.

Sometimes the voice goes after singing 'Sylvia's Mother'.

I do a very emotional version.

The song is about this bitch of a mother trying to get rid of her Sylvia's boyfriend. Lately I've taken to singing 'Sylvia' when I'm sober. Possibly the absence of an oral application of alcohol-based throat muscle relaxant may well have placed extra strain on the vocal chords during the bit where the poor young lad chasing Sylvia sings, "tell her gooood byyyyyye".

14

Welcome Home, Christy, You'll Always Belong Here

November 25, 2013

THE orphan, in his seventies, told the story of how his mother was pregnant and the father wanted nothing to do with her. Her little boy was put into care. For 16 years he lived in a residential home in Tralee in Co Kerry.

His mother and father were both from Kerry. Their names are known to me. And I know the part of Kerry they came from. Here's some of the conversation from the last time we wrote about him, two weeks ago today.

"I don't know where I'm from," he repeated. He was a kindly man. Not in any way obsessive or loud. But he was a bothered man.

"You're a Kerryman," I told him.

"But am I?," he asked. "I was brought up in a home."

"Do you want to be a Kerryman?" I asked. "I always cheer for Kerry in the football," was his reply.

"Well then," I said. "You're a Kerryman. You're one of us."

I promised to set up a meeting with his hero Darragh Ó Sé, but I lost his name and number. We put out a request here for the return of the Kerryman. On Tuesday afternoon the winter sun was low in the sky and, blinded by the glare, I didn't recognise him when he came in to John B's. He didn't say a word. When you've been locked up in a residential home until you're 16, you get to know your place. You do not speak until spoken to.

He asked for a pint and then I knew it was him. He came to see us from Kilmallock in Co Limerick, where he lives now. His name is Christy Quirke and he has a lovely open face. Ever smiling and accepting. But he is sad sometimes, not so much for the man he is now, but for the boy he used to be.

"I was in the home in Tralee for seven years and nobody ever called to see us. Not my mother or my father. No one. It was tough there and we got a good few batens but that was the times that were in it. They were good to us too. Some of them were alright."

There is no sense of bitterness or hate in his gentle voice. Christy holds no grudges. He tried to contact his mother when he left the home in Tralee but "she didn't want to have anything to do with me". He reached out to the man he was certain was his dad. Also a Kerryman. He was told he was not entitled to a paternity test in a letter written by his father's solicitors.

Christy wasn't after money or an inheritance. He just wanted to know for sure who his dad was. All he ever wanted was to be a Kerryman.

I have kin in the area where his father lived. It seems certain Christy was in touch with the right man. How could you turn your back on your own son? I asked. "I suppose," says Christy, "he didn't want me. He had a family of his own and I let it go. I didn't want to cause any trouble."

He left the Monastery Residential Home at 16. Off out into the big world without a penny or a parent or a place to belong to. Christy worked for the McElligotts, who were farmers in Ardfert, near Tralee.

"I was awful happy there and I was stone mad about the little kids. I loved it there too because it was in Kerry." It's easy enough to figure this was the family he always longed to be part of. Christy stayed for five years.

He moved on and his last job was as an "ordinary labourer" in St Joseph's psychiatric hospital in Limerick city.

"I saw everything. My years there taught me to never complain."

In all that time, Christy hardly ever missed a Kerry football game. He married Margaret. They've been together now for 32 years.

"We get on great with each other," says Christy. He has a son and a daughter. He loves them very much. Christy lost another son, tragically, and he's so lonesome for his lost boy.

He is resigned in a calm way to all that life threw at him. But there was that unresolved question.

"Where am I from?"

Christy has been very well looked after and respected in Kilmallock. It's home and he is happy there, but he wants to be one of us – a Kerryman.

"Of course you are Kerry," I told him. Maybe it was the fact that he was rejected by his Kerry parents that in some way made him feel he was unworthy. Christy saw himself as a nobody from the independent republic of nowhere. So sad, and he's being carrying that sense of disconnect for more than 70 years.

Christy loves Darragh Ó Sé. He followed the Kerry team everywhere and even went to Croke Park to see Darragh play for the Gaeltacht but he was too unsure of himself to tell anyone why it was he was following the Kingdom. In case he was told he wasn't really from the Kerry or that he wasn't entitled to cheer for his team.

"Would you talk to Darragh if I put him on the phone?" I asked. His eyes lit up. Darragh and his new pal Christy had a good old chat. I wasn't deliberately listening in but I heard Christy say: "I have nowhere to be from."

Darragh told him he was a Kerryman and "there was no doubt about it". A single pearl-shaped tear rolled slowly down the side of Christy's face.

Darragh is meeting with Christy before Christmas and he is presenting him with a number eight green and gold jersey.

"Do you know now, Christy, where you come from?"

"I do," he replied in a soft voice.

"I'm a Kerryman."

THE BODHRÁN IS ELEMENTAL IRISH PULSE MUSIC. THE BEAT IS US AND OURS. IT'S THE PACEMAKER AT THE HEART OF EVERY TOP-CLASS SESSION. BUT WHEN THE BODHRÁN IS PLAYED BADLY, IT'S WORSE THAN A DENTIST'S DRILL

15

Bungling Bodhránists And A Chronic Outbreak Of Spoons

July 18, 2016

I HAVE declared a vendetta against spoons. It's either them or me. Yesterday was the last day of the Munster Fleadh Cheoil here in Listowel. The finest of Irish traditional music would wear the soles of your shoes from the tapping and the dancing. For the most part.

But if one more lad comes into the pub and takes up a seat for himself, and another one for his giant rucksack, and he doesn't buy a drink and he plays the spoons like a stuck CD track, with his eyes closed, I'll sell the frigging place. I will.

There was this spoonist who was in several times over the weekend and he asked me for the loan of a pair of spoons. We haven't a soup spoon or a dessert spoon left after them. I'd say there are lads going around the place pretending to be spoons players and they are really scrap metal merchants. I'll bet they have a big lorry parked outside towns like Milltown Malbay for Willie Week. That's the Willie Clancy Summer School. Which reminds us of the story of the man who tried to pay a compliment to a woman fiddler playing at the famous West Clare festival.

"Your tune made my Willie Week," he said, full of emotion.

"I hope it gets better soon," she said.

I made up that one myself, but it could have happened.

I couldn't sleep last night even though I was worn out. It was the spoons, the spoons. I'd gladly swap beds with The Hunchback of Notre Dame. The staccato clickety-clack kept on playing in my head and it wouldn't go away.

I YouTubed Handel's 'Water Music' on a loop, which only had me getting up to go to the toilet every 10 minutes, such is the power of suggestion on the subconscious.

It was like having your bed beside the train tracks in Heuston Station.

The spoon player asked me for the spoons in the middle of a session from some incredible musicians led by Lillie Morris from Augusta, Georgia, who came all the way to Listowel to play for us and launch her superb art exhibition.

I gave him spoons. Plastic ones. Borrowed from Jumbo's, where they have lovely food.

Then he asked me for a pint of MiWadi. Well it's not really a pint of MiWadi, which would kill you with the sweetness, but a drop of MiWadi in a pint glass.

So I charge him a euro, which I never do. The unit cost is small enough.

We often give pints out to poor poets and the like at Writers' Week as part of our 'Billy Keane sponsors the arts' programme.

The spoon player goes mad and says: "You're charging spoons players for MiWadi."

As if I was after painting a moustache on the Mona Lisa. He went off in several huffs and the musicians thanked me.

It was a bit sad not having Bert Griffin about the place. Bert passed away in October and we laid his ashes down with his parents. He kept Irish music going in London for years in his pub, The Stag's Head. So proud I was when I was asked to say the few words by Conor, Tara and Paula at my friend's graveside last Sunday.

I could fill the paper every day this week with stories about Bert. He would argue on any topic – and sometimes for the sake of the debate, Bert would disagree with himself – but what a big heart he had and he was always great sport.

Every Christmas Day, Bert would host a big dinner for men without family in London. Taxis were sent to hostels and homes.

That was Bert, and he never saw an Irish person stuck. Poor Bert hadn't much time for spoons players or the bodhrán chancers who hijack sessions.

The bodhrán is elemental Irish pulse music. The beat is us and ours. It's the pacemaker at the heart of every top-class session. But when the bodhrán is played badly, it's worse than a dentist's drill.

Séamus Ennis, the famous uilleann piper, was asked one time what was the best way to play a bodhrán. The animal-skin drum is usually tapped by hand or with a wooden one-piece. Séamus's answer was "with a pen knife".

This American bodhrán player ruined a good few sessions over the weekend. He was nice, though, and earnest. We didn't want to hurt his feelings. He joined in and it was like a TV licence inspector banging on the door.

Some of the younger musicians were truly incredible. There's great hope for our country and our music. Most of them were competing.

The competitions are intense and the standard is the very highest. Munster medals are hard won. All-Irelands are really world championships.

Years of practice go into the makings of a champion. The young uilleann pipers work away for decades before they are ready for solos and concerts.

But spoon players are ready to go in a second.

It's time to go down to work in the pub. I'm feeling sorry now. Sorry I was so hard on the spoons player. He was very annoyed when I gave him the plastic spoons, again, on his return after the earlier walk-out.

"No one will hear these yokes," he said bitterly. "Don't worry," says I. "Plastic spoons are the new air guitar." And I mixed him a MiWadi on the house.

> ## "DO YOU MIKEY TAKE MARY TO BE YOUR LAWFUL WIFE?" MIKEY REPLIES: "I DO, BUT TERMS AND CONDITIONS APPLY"

| 16 |

The Farmer Wants A Wife And Solicitor For A Pre-nup Agreement

October 28, 2013

I T'S all about the economics of love. Says the farmer: "You go up to the altar with a 100 acres and you come back down with 50. You're not just saying 'I do' to marrying the man or woman you love. That 'I do' means, 'I do be after giving you 20 of the 40 cows, one-and-a-half spears from the three-prong pike and the hind legs of Rover the border collie'."

So it is on this blustery Sunday morning, instead of passing the winter-time extra hour in bed with love making, the young farmer will be worrying about what will happen to the land if he marries his sweetheart. His parents are wary of the daughter-in-law anyway, but it's 10 times worse when Your Wan could end up with half the family farm.

Herself spent 40 years, slaving away, worrying about money, milking cows, piking out dung and feeding scoury calves out of a bucket before dawn on freezing February mornings. The money for the bit of style is gone to pay for bales of hay, while Your Wan has an extra hour in bed every morning and not just on clock-changing Sunday. She's able to keep long purple nails and her hands are as soft as silk. There isn't a chilblain on her face. The son's girl goes spinning in the gym and asks for a skinny latte at supper. She wants to live in the town, in a house with three bathrooms. And worse again Your Wan is taking advantage of the innocent son as was evidenced when Herself found a box of French Tickler condoms in the glove compartment of the Massey.

So that's the mother's side and here's more from her.

"I could've left plenty of times and claimed my share but I wanted to keep the farm in one piece for my son and now all she has to do is get up and go and she can take my half with her." Farms will not be signed over to sons and daughters for fear of marital break ups. CSO figures show that only 6.2pc of farmers are under 35 and 26.3pc are over 65. That is a decline of 52.8pc in numbers under 35 years from 2000 to 2010. So reports an excellent Macra na Feirme paper from Dr Pat Bogue. There are other reasons, too. Farming is hard work and a bad winter or disease can finish off a family farm.

So it is we are in grave danger of going back to the old days when courtships lasted forever. There's the one about the couple who were walking out for 17 years. Mary finally plucks up enough courage to ask: "Do you think Mikey that we should maybe start thinking about getting married?" Mikey's cheeks contract as he sucks the value out of the last of the wine gum. Finally he says: "Sure Mary, who would want to marry the likes of us?"

The Irish Farmers' Association (IFA) is lobbying for a law to ensure pre-nuptial agreements are legally binding. The legal position is unclear at the moment.

So now we might have our very own Irish menage-a-trois. The farmer, his lover and the solicitor.

So who are the gold-diggers and who are the genuine?

The old system was the dowry.

The money was handed over by the woman for the privilege of working for a lifetime on a farm over which she had no legal right. Farms were never signed over to the dowry women. I was there the day the dowry died. My friend told me he was made ask Your Wan for a dowry by Herself, his mother. Your Wan stripped off. There was no talk of money after that.

But it was the mothers who eventually put an end to the dowry system. Women were treated as chattels until relatively recent times.

It wasn't until 1965 that Charlie Haughey passed a law ensuring a legal right share for the widow if her husband cut her out of the will.

I know too there were fine men who treated their wives very well.

Those mothers of 1940s, 50s, 60s and even 70s Ireland, who were not so well-minded, were going to make sure their daughters didn't suffer the same fate. These women reared their girls to be strong and independent.

To the IFA I would say, love does count for something and asking a woman to sign a pre-nup is about as romantic as giving her a washer for an engagement ring.

Women have choices and chances now their mothers and grandmothers never had. What about the case of the woman who does sign a pre-nup? Will she be kicked out in years to come if the husband decides to trade her in. Your Wan will have become Herself. What rights will Herself have then after her years of unpaid toil?

You can sort of see the IFA side of it, too. Farms aren't like bank accounts. You can't just count up the money and divide it neatly in two. Most farmers could not afford to pay half the monetary value of the farm in cash. Half a farm would be nearly always too small to be economically viable, around where I live anyway. There's the emotional investment, too. Men and women worked for decades to keep landlords and banks at bay. To keep the land for future generations. To keep it one piece. They love the land itself; the grass, the trees, the ditches and the hedges.

This is a drama that will be acted out all over rural Ireland today and in the years ahead.

Here's Act II. The happy couple finally make it to the altar. The priest asks for the consent.

"Do you Mikey take Mary to be your lawful wife?" Mikey replies: "I do, but terms and conditions apply."

MY FATHER WROTE *THE FIELD* IN 1965. THE STAGE VERSION AND THE SUBSEQUENT MOVIE WERE LARGELY INFLUENCED BY THE EVENTS OF NOVEMBER 1958

17

The Field - Retracing The Murder Of Maurice Moore

February, 2013

MAURICE MOORE was murdered in November 1958. Dan Foley was the chief suspect. Dan was never charged with the Moore murder, but he was found guilty by his friends and neighbours. Dan Foley was sentenced to death by isolation. He died a lonely and broken man, just five years after the death of his closest neighbour.

The killing took place in the Reamore hill country, just seven miles from Tralee, and the case captured the front pages for weeks, back in the days when there were only a couple of murders committed in the state every year.

Yet the killing would have been long forgotten if a young writer had passed on an invite from a friend to take a drive up to the murder location. My father wrote The Field in 1965. The stage version and the subsequent movie were largely influenced by the events of November 1958. My mother tells of how Dad returned home from the scene of the murder and he just couldn't get it out of his head for days after.

My father saw the huge frame of the dark, brooding Dan Foley through the window of his house and the effect it had on him led to the creation of The Bull McCabe. Foley though was only the physical manifestation of The Bull who was mostly conceived in John B's fertile and relentless imagination.

Dan's nephew John criticised John B who felt Dan Foley was the killer but only divulged this long after Dan died. My dad was well got on the hill country. Most of the locals are sure Foley did it.

I visited John's home and the man couldn't have been more welcoming.

"My uncle Dan was framed," he says, "and I can prove it."

We go through the evidence for and against Dan Foley.

Dan Foley and Maurice Moore were due in Tralee Circuit Court just a month or so after the killing. The dispute concerned a 400 metre long and narrow strip of land which Moore alleged was taken over by Foley.

Moore initiated the proceedings and Dan Foley, says nephew John, defended the matter in full, stating he actually owned the land that was fenced in by his ditch.

"He was sure he would win the case," pleads John, "so why kill Moss Moore when he would be the obvious suspect?"

We visited Paul Reidy in the course of the investigation. Paul, a sprightly 77-year-old, took us through the barren, wild landscape of the Foley and Moore farms. He lives just a few hundred metres from the murder scene. His memory of the events of 1958 is near perfect.

Paul is a friendly, open man and he co-operated fully with us.

He maintains Dan Foley told him: "There would be one person showing up at the court case."

Paul told of meeting Dan Foley's wife who told him Moore was gone off working in Tipperary and he also informed the Gardai of meeting Foley on the road around the day after Moore went missing. Foley, he says, had a cut on his face.

John Foley, who wouldn't have much time for Paul Reidy, maintains this was a result of 'a puck from a cow'.

Paul was adamant Dan Foley was the murderer. He was going to tell the truth and didn't 'give a damn' what John Foley was going to say.

Fifty four years on and the bitterness is still there.

Two decent men, who in the ordinary course of events might have been friends and neighbours, are on opposite sides of a battle for posthumous justice.

John is convinced Moss Moore was murdered for money. Paul, who was a close friend of Moss Moore's, confirmed Moore sold livestock and could have had money in his possession, but it was unlikely if he was a wealthy man on a farm that could only hold five or six cows.

John Foley says his uncle left nearly £13,000 at the time of his death, a huge sum at the time and that money was therefore never a motive for Dan. John didn't have any documentary evidence of this in his possession when I visited his home.

It took the searchers eight days to find Moss Moore's body just a few yards from his house, tucked well in under an overhanging ditch in a fast flowing stream.

We visited the scene.

"That's my land," says John. "Ye were trespassing." But he doesn't make an issue of it, other than to state the fact.

We uncovered new hearsay evidence from an eyewitness who told her children: "Foley went crazy when he heard the news the body had been found. He was very agitated and was going mad around the kitchen."

John Foley looks me straight in the eye. He believes what he is saying to be true. "My uncle was drinking out of the stream where the body was found and this was why he was so angry."

A local source, who wishes to remain anonymous, told us Dan did have a clean water supply. If only the dead could talk.

Indeed Dan Foley refused to talk to anyone and this in itself was taken as a sign of his guilt but the law back in 1958 was that the right to silence was sacrosanct and could not be commented upon in a subsequent trial.

The legal advice given to suspects back then was to keep their mouths shut on the basis that sometimes even innocent people can inadvertently incriminate themselves.

Garda Kavanagh used to cut turf up on the mountain with Moore and Foley.

The garda said Moore sent word Foley was following him home at night. Garda Kavanagh was busy and didn't get there in time. In fairness, Kavanagh would have had to cycle seven miles uphill to get to the murder scene. The Garda, now deceased, speaking on the excellent TG4 documentary 'Fuil agus Duch' said this was his greatest regret. A kindly man, he also said he would leave it to God to decide the identity of the murderer.

Up to now it was assumed Moore was a small man of about 10 stones but we have seen evidence taken from the original autopsy. Moore weighed anything up to 11st 7lbs which is for and against Dan Foley. His detractors might say Foley was a big strong man and it would have taken a big man to throttle Moss Moore. His voice box was broken. More might say there was more than one involved in the murder.

What does seem likely is that the culprit was a local. The night of the murder was as black as coal. It's rough terrain, in off the road, and you would want to know your way around. The place where the body was found must have been known to the killer. It would be nigh on impossible for a stranger to pick such a secure hiding place in the wet, pitch-black Reamore night.

Moore carried a flash lamp with him on his way home from a card game on his last night alive.

The flash lamp was found in Dan Foley's turnip garden, just a few yards from his house.

John Foley argues it was planted there by a member of the gardai now deceased. "It would have been a stupid place for my uncle to hide the lamp," says John. We have discovered no evidence to back up this assertion.

Sources close to the garda investigation reveal for the first time that a lone garda, now dead, approached Foley without informing his colleagues. Foley was then ready when the Dublin detectives called to interview him.

Dan Foley's file was returned from the Attorney-General with a one line decision – 'insufficient evidence.'

Paul Reidy who spent eight days looking for the body with Moore's dogs Smallie and Spring was also surprised.

"We all knew Foley did it."

"Sometimes someone comes up and asks me about the murder and I just ..." Paul makes a choking clicking noise and twists his neck. He laughs: "That doesn't be long sending them off about their business."

John Foley was in his uncle's house when a volley of shots was fired through the window. "It was definitely an attempt to kill my uncle and whoever happened to be in the house."

Our investigation has discovered that a bomb was planted on a ditch opposite the Foley house. No great damage was done. We have been told one of the perpetrators worked in a quarry and was familiar with gelignite. Another was a man of limited intelligence who boasted to a neighbour:"We blew the f****r all the way to Macca (a nearby mountain)."

My father received a late night phone call to Listowel 66 after he closed the pub around the time the play version of 'The Field' was first produced.

He was threatened that if the play went on he would be bombed. My mother was adamant the show would go on.

So is Dan Foley a murderer? For sure he's the chief suspect, but would a jury find him guilty?

There was no forensic evidence. Incredibly there was a wake in Moore's home after the murder rendering all of the fingerprints as contaminated evidence. If money was a motive and it was hidden in the house, there was no way of proving it.

Ciaran Cassidy, producer of 'Fuil agus Duch', whose mother came from the mountain, summed it up best: "There are no absolutes in Reamore."

A jury would most likely have acquitted Foley even if the case did go to trial. But there's no reasonable doubt in the court of the vigilante.

There were two casualties on that fateful November night in 1958. One was Moss Moore, the other was Dan Foley. Dan died alone from a heart attack just yards from where Moss Moore's body was found. John Foley says the stress of the boycott killed him.

Mrs Foley lived out her days with Dan's brother, Mick, who was crippled from arthritis. In former times Mick entertained the ramblers with his concertina but there were no visitors other than close family and Paul Reidy's wife who was good to Mrs Foley.

Paul Reidy who went to so much trouble to show us around the killing field is still grieving for Moss Moore.

John Foley mourns for his uncle.

There are beautiful new houses just beyond the murder scene on the right-hand side as you walk up from the main road. On the side where the killing took place all that remains is the nearly inaccessible ruin of Moore's house. There's hardly a trace of the Foley home.

The small farms where they slaved are sad places now.

The land is overgrown "and only fit for snipe." Forestry covers some of the Moore farm. As a point of honour John Foley bought back the family land.

There's a terrible, atmospheric sadness in this forlorn spot where such terrible events occurred over half a century ago. It seeps under the skin. The very land is anaemic. No birdsong here in this bleak place or playing children as in days of yore. No neighbours calling for talk and tea. It's as if Mick's concertina is playing a requiem for the dead.

We find an old bottle and a jam jar washed up by the winter floods close to the spot where the body was found. Maybe Dan and Moss shared a drink with bread and jam in the days when they were friends.

So much lost, so many lives destroyed and for so little.

After all the strife on the high coarse meadows of their beloved mountain, Dan Foley and Moss Moore were left with just two tablecloth burial plots. In separate graveyards.

18

Rural Ireland's Not Dead And Gone – It's Adapting And Battling

March 31, 2014

THE old cobbler's shop at the front of the family home hasn't changed in 40 years. An old Singer sewing machine is stationed by the window for the light. Shoes in various states of repair are upended on benches covered with leather trimmings and the cobbler's surgical instruments.

The Templemore cobbler, Liam Brewer, is getting on and he's not in the best of health.

Liam tells us his business is in decline. "People can buy cheap shoes and the cost of repairs is too much."

But the ones who know and respect perfect craftsmanship come from far and wide to the Cobbler of Templemore.

"I'll keep going as long as I can," says Liam.

"The kidney function is down to 23pc now. It'll not be long before I have to go on the dialysis."

There is hope for small towns in that the remaining businesses have survived the worst recession ever. Lessons have been learned.

The Garda College was closed down a few years back and the loss of 800 recruits nearly finished Templemore. Businesses went bust and one poor man was left with the four empty houses he bought to billet recruits at a rate of €65 per student per week. The college is re-opening soon, with a 100-student intake to begin with. The sudden and unexpected closing down is a lesson for all of us.

Most small towns are dependent on 'the factory', the one big industry that sustains the whole place. The danger here is if the factory closes, then the town goes down with it. The key could be the support of smaller indigenous businesses so that if one fails the whole place isn't affected by the aftershock. The future is bright, though. Most of us love our home places. Now is the time for practical patriots.

We meet our friend and guide, the talkative Ronan Loughnane, who describes himself as "a stay-at-home dad" ever since he was made redundant a few years back. "Are you frustrated over being unemployed?" we ask.

"Are you joking me?" replies Ronan. "Sure I was there outside the old job last summer and I saw the lads going in to work for a long shift on a sunny day and I says to myself, there's a lot to be said for minding children and making the dinner." Ronan sells himself short. He works hard for the community and the GAA in particular.

These men and women who give up so much of their time to help their home places are often taken for granted. Very often the running of the likes of the Tidy Towns, the GAA and the helping out with the church are left to the few who really care. Everyone should lend a hand if small town Ireland is to thrive.

Ronan maintains the secret to Templemore's staying alive is the evolving chemistry between the natives and the new people, who come in to town. "The newcomers wake us up," he says. "There's great go in them." The old insulting term of 'blow-ins' is often used in small towns to refer to non-natives but small places need constant renewal if they are to survive.

Ronan's brother Cuilan brews White Gypsy ruby ale. The pot-bellied copper stills are gleaming. The smell of hops and wheat would drive you to drink. The beer is beautiful to the taste with a lovely snow-white creamy head, a red-black colour down below and a lingering hoppy aftertaste.

Cuilan's Welsh wife Sally does all the book work and his pal Jamie Groome delivers the beer and cleans the lines. In return, the left over mash from the brewing process is fed to Jamie's pigs.

The success story is one of having the bottle to give it a go, producing top-quality organic produce, keeping costs down, hard work and getting the community behind you. Most of the pubs in the area stock the local brew. White Gypsy is a template for all of small town Ireland.

It hasn't all been all plain sailing. "Ronan and myself brought a beer to be tried out by a pub in Dublin. It was extra strong and we drank too much. I was in a heap. We only made fairly handy strength beers after that."

The farmers keep us going. Templemore is a market town. The farmers call to the post offices and have Mass cards signed for the dead and the living. Shopping local is vital for survival.

We call to Centenary Thurles Stores, part of a farmers' co-op, and the manager Donal O'Dwyer tells us business is improving, "especially in the last six months". He makes an interesting observation.

"The small builders with three or four men working for them are still in business," he says. "They have plenty of work on right now. The farmers have come through the fodder crisis and the bad weather of last year. If you're good at something, then you'll survive."

This is the key. We must up our game in the small towns. There's no point on waiting for the IDA or the politicians to do it for us. The townspeople must be independent and get these small businesses up and running. And we must be very good at what we do.

Claire Walsh is back home from Cork for her mother Mary's birthday. Claire is engaged and we ask her if she would like to come back here for good. Claire tells us her native place would be a lovely area in which to rear a family. That's the biggest test passed. Small towns are very family friendly with good and free schools, less expensive housing, relations for baby-sitting and a short commute.

"There's plenty to do in small towns but you have to go out and look for it," says Sean Ryan, the director of the Templemore Drama Society. "The fun won't find you sitting at home."

The small town is the best place then to rear a family. Start planning now for the homecoming. Dreams and ideas often come true. You can run a business from anywhere and think of the joy, if your plan can bring jobs back home.

For sure there are problems. The kids leave secondary school and very few come back home to settle. The recession stole away our young people but right now I'll bet there's a native son or daughter in Oz planning a business that will revitalise their native place.

There is a realisation that unless we battle to stay alive the constant promotion of the city-state, and online shopping will close us down. The unimaginative will cut services like our post offices first rather than take the time to grow rural Ireland. It's all about guts, brains and an unrelenting loyalty to people and place.

The lines of Abraham Lincoln somehow come to mind. "I like to see a man proud of the place in which he lives. I like to see a man live so that his place will be proud of him."

19

The Pain – And Fun –
Of Saying Goodbye
While You're Still Here...

April 28, 2014

THIS is the true story of Paddy Joe Keane, the man who attended his own wake while he was still alive.

Paddy Joe's farewell was a traditional Irish wake with lashings of drink and a sing-song. But even Paddy couldn't cheat death and three weeks after the living wake, hundreds of mourners paid tribute to a brave and funny man who finally lost his battle with lung cancer. Paddy Joe was a 40-a-day man and in the end it was the cigarettes that got him. He was only 53.

Paddy Joe lived in Killenard in Co Laois, the puck of a five iron away from the palatial Heritage Golf and Spa club.

His widow Bernie welcomed me to her comfortable home. The tea was made and we were told Paddy Joe's father was a Kerryman. In an amazing coincidence it seems we are far out cousins.

Her husband died over two years ago, but, Bernie says: "I still wait for him to come in the door."

"He was mad, but in a good way. Paddy Joe always made me laugh and he had a great oul' brain. He thought of things other people couldn't do. Didn't he climb up that tree there outside the house and put up a bird box. He could do anything with his hands."

Paddy Joe was in the army and worked as a caretaker in a local hotel until the recession struck. The couple have three children and son Paddy comes in from cutting the grass. "Paddy Joe was gas," says his son. "He loved a good piss-up and he told us the thought of us all drinking away without him at the wake would kill him. That was the way he talked."

Says Bernie: "He was even going to bring in a coffin and get up out of it with a drink in his hand."

"He was only winding you up, Mam," adds Paddy. But Paddy Joe was serious about having the wake.

"He was a great man for Facebook and he contacted all his friends." Bernie still laughs at her husband's carry-on. "Paddy Joe was told he only had a few weeks left. He said to us right here in the house: 'I don't want everyone to be at the wake when I can't be at it myself.'"

She laughs all the time when she talks about him. You could see that was why she fell for him when they met in a pub over 30 years ago. The Thatch is only a few minutes' walk up the hill from the Keane family home and the pub was packed for Paddy Joe's big night. It was your typical wake. Half celebration for a life lived, and half lament for a life lost. Paddy Joe pumped himself up with his secret stash of steroids. He smoked his share of cigarettes and drank a good few pints of Bud. Says Paddy: "Dad wanted for us to be happy with him. He got us into a place where we were all comfortable."

Paddy Joe and Bernie even went out dancing. "It was our last dance," she recalls and the tears come now.

Paddy Joe planned the wake meticulously. "One of his favourite songs was Roger Whittaker's 'The Last Farewell' and he went up on stage with the band to sing that one," recalls Paddy.

Paddy Joe's sister Rose had the band play 'He Ain't Heavy, He's My Brother', and they had the place rocking and swaying. He joined his sister Nuala in a song sung in Irish.

Friends came up to the family like you would at a wake for a dead person. One woman said "he'd do anything for anyone". It was a sort of an alive sorry for your troubles. Paddy couldn't handle his Dad's farewell speech. He had to go outside for a smoke. His Dad thanked everyone for coming and bade his friends goodbye. He finished up with: "I love everyone here."

The mourners were in tears. Paddy Joe didn't cry. He went back to his pint, his smokes and his jokes. Paddy Joe kicked on, full belt, until one o'clock. He was worn out by then. He had no more to give.

Paddy Joe wasn't a wealthy man. He gathered together a precious and varied collection of CDs and he divided up his music between his children a few days after the wake.

He died on February 16, 2012, just three weeks after the last night in The Thatch. He was brave and cheerful, but this time the wake was for real.

So why did Paddy Joe decide he would be the chief celebrant at his own wake? He was fond of the drink and he loved to talk. That much we do know. Bernie is very much in love with Paddy Joe. The memory of that last party keeps her laughing. She sees the wake as her man's last fling. No more than that.

The walls of the house are decorated with Paddy's pyrography. The burnt images on timber were presents for his family. Paddy has inherited his father's gifted hands. He knows what his Dad was up to.

We drive to Portarlington where Paddy lives now and he tells us the why.

"Paddy Joe knew we would be heartbroken. He was taking the pressure off the funeral. Paddy Joe was guiding us through to his death.

"Paddy Joe loved the laugh of it all and the session but I think the wake was just his way of saying I'm off and I'll be all right and so will ye.

"My take is, Paddy Joe was saying to his family and friends, the memories of the last stand will keep me alive and keep ye happy."

Paddy Joe Keane, the clever handyman from Killenard, might just have figured out a new and better way of dying.

LIFE CAN DEFEAT US ON POINTS OR BY KNOCKOUT. THE SECRET IS TO FIND A WAY TO KEEP GOING. TO FIND A REASON FOR WHAT IT IS THAT HAS CHANGED YOUR LIFE FOREVER OR TO FIND A CAUSE WORTH FIGHTING FOR

| 20 |

Men Must Change Their Way Of Thinking – We Owe It To Jill Meagher

May 5, 2014

HE was anxious there in the Green Room, just before 'The Late Late Show'. You could see Tom Meagher just wanted to get out there like maybe a football player in the tunnel before a big game.

Tom Meagher was about to tell his country the terrible story of how his beloved wife Jill was raped and murdered in Australia.

I have this picture in my head of Tom and Jill together. It is not a real picture in the sense that I had never met Tom and Jill as a couple. It's just an imagined scene. They are walking hand in hand, happy and relaxed in each other's company. You do an immediate, quick audit as we do sometimes on a streetscape and think: "Man, they're so good looking together. They have it all."

Life can defeat us on points or by knockout. The secret is to find a way to keep going. To find a reason for what it is that has changed your life forever or to find a cause worth fighting for. Tom Meagher is doing his best to make sense of the horrific rape and murder of his lovely wife and Tom Meagher has found a cause.

White Ribbon is a worldwide movement designed to end violence by men against women. The figures are truly frightening. One in three women suffer violence at the hands of men. Nearly all of us know of a woman who has been a victim of violence. Most men are truly appalled by men's violence against women. But we do have some responsibility to bear.

"Did you hear the one about the hooker ..." so goes the opening line of a 'joke'. Do you say "stop it right there", or do you acquiesce in the telling of a story that dehumanises the prostitute by the very act of listening? I'm sorry to say I would have heard many so-called jokes over many years and just listened, uncomfortably, but without any rebuke to the teller. That's a big part of what White Ribbon is about. A big part of what Tom Meagher is trying to change.

I promised Tom I would write about his cause today but all week I struggled to get the import of what he is saying. But then it dawns on you that our words define us and the words we choose to listen to and leave unchallenged also make us what we are.

When we tell jokes or support the telling of such stories by simply listening or even forcing a laugh from a sort of misplaced sense of masculine social etiquette, our very being there and doing nothing makes us very much part of the problem. What may just be a casual telling of a dirty joke to a group of men can trivialise violence to women.

The retelling all over the world a billion times over creates a template for those on the verge of acting out violent tendencies towards women. The years of build-up of such talk lodge until the perpetrators of violence against women see their actions as justified and the norm.

Tom's blog on White Ribbon.com was published here a few days ago. It is an emotional but very well-thought-out testament to his belief that words and attitudes are accessories to the murder and rape of women. The old wartime warning "loose talk costs lives" very much applies.

We will quote from Tom on whiteribbonblog.com. "We see instances of this occur in bars when men become furious and verbally abusive to, or about, women who decline their attention. We see it on the street as groups of men shout comments, grab, grope and intimidate women with friends either ignoring or getting involved in the activity. We see it in male peer groups where rape jokes and disrespectful attitudes towards women go uncontested."

I saw it in a town in the west this week. A boy tried to grope a youngster. She pushed him away and didn't seem to mind too much but I sensed it was because she had no support. The other boys just let it be.

I would respectfully suggest that if you have a son, Tom's blog should be given to him to read over. Read it yourself. Most of us just don't realise the harm that is being caused. Tom tells of the first time he heard his wife's murderer speak in coherent sentences. He reasoned then that 'the monster myth' which explains away all violence against woman as being the act of a deranged, inhuman evil-doer is the easy way out for us men.

But it all starts somewhere. Maybe even on the side of a sunny street in the west of Ireland. If we men can change our way of thinking and the attitude of the men we socialise with, the positive effect will in some way help Tom Meagher and in some way make it up to his beloved Jill.

I COULD NEVER SEE THE SENSE BEHIND THE CONCEPT OF COMPULSORY CELIBACY. TOTAL ABSTINENCE JUST CANNOT BE BENEFICIAL FOR A PERSON'S HEALTH

Singletons Are Being Condemned To Live As Born-again Virgins

June 23, 2014

VIRGINS would be scarce enough nowadays but there is no shortage of born-again virgins. The church kept the numbers up for years, of the originals, that is. The few virgins we have left now in Ireland wouldn't fill up the front few pews and so it has come to pass that the ranks of the virgins have been boosted by the inclusion of the born-agains.

The message from the church was to lay off the sex until you get married. Keep yourself for the big day and you will be fully compliant. There are millions of Catholics all over the world of a certain age who believed they would be doomed if they went off before the starter's gun, which was usually fired late at night in the hotel room and the level of expertise was often of a very poor standard due to lack of practice.

It would have been easier to persuade T Rex to turn vegetarian.

Although a limo driver – whom it must be said is prone to exaggeration in that he claims to have taken Elvis from Shannon to Feakle some five years after the king was declared dead – told me the story of the couple who consummated their marriage in the course of the journey from the church to the hotel, a trip of some three miles. It could be, as was often the case in the old days, that a long engagement was effectively 20 years of foreplay.

I could never see the sense behind the concept of compulsory celibacy. Total abstinence just cannot be beneficial for a person's health. Just look at the fallout from the misdeeds of our biggest congregation of virgins. There is no doubt but that child sex abuse is linked to the prohibition on sex for the clergy.

The question of choice is paramount. Many young people will wait until the big day. Fair enough, if that is what they want. There are the terms of conditions such as the age of consent that must be complied with and sexual safety must be adhered to at all times. It would be best if there was love and respect involved in the relationship but aside from these prerequisites, I wouldn't see any great harm in young or old people having sex.

The younger people, for the most part, do have a choice but what about the born-again virgins who have gone so long without sex that their virginal status has been regained. I hear so many stories of attractive and intelligent women from late thirties on who live the life of virgins. Many of the women are divorced and on the nights when the kids are with the father they stay at home watching TV, all alone, drinking wine, which is not good for body or soul.

Such is modern Ireland. The liberation of divorce has become an enslavement. The lonely are scared of losing their anonymity by joining a dating agency. As we have often written here, Ireland is too small for secrets and there is the danger that the mother might be caught trying to get dates online by their own nosy kids.

One very attractive 40-something woman explained her situation. "I can't go to a bar or club on my own. I know I should try but you feel everyone is looking at you. There are married women then who think you might be after their husbands or that you are in some way desperate. It is so hard to find someone. It's not even that we are looking for a date. Just to be in men's company and have a bit of fun is enough.

"Sometimes I do go out with my friend. We just sit there and look at each other. Then I get to thinking, I've just spent €70 on the night out and all I'm doing is looking at my friend. Now what I do on Friday nights is I put the €70 in a jar and I think at least I can go on holiday and meet men in Spain where there is no shortage. I live for that week every year."

I suggested a website for women who are not gay and just want a friend as a wing woman but the attractive 40-something says women are less likely to get on in such situations as two men who travel out and about. So naturally I ask why this is the case.

"Women are planners and then if one woman is chatted up and the other isn't, she doesn't know what to do with herself. Men just wander off around a bar and leave their friend with a woman, but we can't because that's just the way it is. It's easy for men, they can initiate the conversation with women, but if we wander around on your own randomly chatting up men, well then we're looked on as some sort of whore.

"Then by the time you get to your forties and you are divorced or single, you find most of the good men are already snapped up anyway. And the single ones do not really want a woman with kids. But it's not like we desperately need a permanent companion. A date would be nice."

It's sad, isn't it, that so many fine women in the prime of their lives are left without. We need a change of attitude by the lonely women and by society in general.

I know of one or two married women who always make sure they bring along their single friends to social engagements. This really is a woman's problem that can only be solved by women.

The women of Ireland need to talk this through and come up with solutions to help out the sisterhood. Ireland is a country where thousands of our women are being denied the right to love and be loved.

The plight of lonely women has been ignored for far too long.

IF ONLY I HAD TOLD
JOHN'S MOTHER THE TRUTH,
WE MIGHT HAVE BEEN ABLE
TO BRING HIM BACK HOME
FOR HIS FINAL YEARS.
AND SHE WOULD HAVE
HAD SOME PEACE

| 22 |

Far From Home – But Close To A Mum's Heart

September 24, 2012

IT has always been this way. Nearly all of my school pals emigrated. For a while in TigerTime I thought emigration was a thing of the past. There's a goodbye party every weekend in our town. Now my kids' pals are nearly all gone abroad. Handsome and pretty they are, brilliant and full of personality. I thought I'd never see the day and it breaks my heart.

There's Skype, cheaper travel, the net and a massive back-up of friends abroad. There is the dignity of work and the fine weather. But it's not home.

One day, a good few years ago, I spotted three down-and-outs roasting spuds in the embers of a fire near a fruit-and-veg depot in London's financial district. I gave the old boys a few coins for a bottle of Chateaux Monday and as I walked away a voice came as if from a dream: "I'm from Listowel. Co Kerry."

That's my home place.

We'll call him John and he was the caricature of a tramp with grey skin, a long white beard and unkempt hair. He was wearing smelly, old, outsize charity clothes and his sad eyes were vacant bloodshot slits under bushy eyebrows. We chatted and I knew his mother. She was in her 80s at the time.

John was staying in a nearby hostel. The drink and rough living had dimmed his thought processes.

Jerry Epstein, a wealthy Jewish-American film producer, did his best to look after the broken-down Irish man. Jeremiah O'Carroll, a friend from here living in London, called to see the poor fella most Saturdays and was very good to him.

Then one day, John vanished. That's what they do when you get too close and it was about three years before I came across John for the final time.

In the meantime I did my research. John's father was a well-to-do businessman and his mother came from a poor family. The businessman ignored John's mother after he got her pregnant. The mother brought him up as best she could. John was a handsome young lad. He drank but not to excess. The mother asked John's father for financial help on the eve of their son's departure for England. He chased John and his mammy out of the big house.

John went to London. He was a good worker but like many more he drank too much, due to loneliness, or possibly the rejection by his father. Bit by bit, the drink took over.

I asked an old friend of John's mother for advice. We came to the conclusion we would not tell her about the meeting in London. She was very old and the upset would be too much for her. It was easier that way for me.

John did come home – in a small box, 40 or more years after he left Ireland on a big ship.

I closed the door of my pub as the small funeral cortege was pulling its way slowly up William Street. That's the custom around here. As the funeral passed the bar window there was John's mother sitting in the front seat of the hearse.

I met her on the street a day or two later. "Sorry," I said. She was crying. "Ah but Billy, if only I knew where he was."

My heart sank.

I know the Irish abroad are very good to the fallen. If all else fails, contact parents or family back home before it's too late. The culture of keeping quiet must end. There are times when what goes on tour must go home.

If only I had told John's mother the truth, we might have been able to bring him back home for his final years. And she would have had some peace.

Such is the stuff of forever regret, and that irreversible 'if only' still haunts me, more than 20 years on.

| 23 |

August – When Love And Holiday Lust Come To The Fore

August 4, 2014

A MAN from the west told me that August was the start of the conceiving season in his part of the world. The economics of his island decided that most of the men had to hit off to London for work. Back home they came, around now, for the builders' holidays. They more than made up for the enforced economic chastity through absence. The only contraception permitted by Church or State was a feed of drink. There was some talk of a contraceptive system called the rhythm method but it was complicated with takings of temperatures and the making of ovarian cycle charts.

You can imagine the homecoming. The father and mother have done without since Christmas, the wintertime conceiving festival, or maybe even longer, if the money was too tight for the making of a trip back home. There wouldn't be time for much examining of charts or reading thermometers when the husband came home from England. It was straight into action and could you blame them? I'd say that first night was eagerly awaited and lustfully consummated.

When I was a boy, the working men would come from England to see their families and friends. We loved to see them coming and they partied like there was no going back. I was young and didn't realise that they would have to work hard in tough conditions for the rest of the year. I used to think they lived it up all year round at home and abroad. My Dad knew what it was like to go back to England after the holidays and he would get very lonesome after his friends. But the custom of living it up in August has been established even if there are too many building workers who have 52 weeks holidays every year.

Love and holiday lust will come to the fore, what with the few drinks and the long lie-ins. There will be couples in mobile homes where the acoustics are far too good and the wall insulation is no thicker than a lettuce leaf who will be sending the children to the pictures or the amusement arcades. Fathers will empty their pockets to ensure the children will stay away long enough.

The children will be hyper for the rest of the day, but it's a small price to pay for minutes of stolen passion.

The condition is known as CSB. It's a terrible dose and as bad an affliction as could befall a man, if it's not caught in time. The sap rises in August and the CSB has been known to affect the finely calibrated margins that control the conduits of the mind and send thoughts and imaginings flowing from rocky rapids to still, calm pools.

You will not find CSB in the medical books. Nor is there any support group for sufferers, especially in August, when the doctors and therapists go on holidays. August is the toughest month for CSB sufferers. The harvest moons pull the oceans back and forth as easily as cutlery drawers. You can only imagine the torment caused by the tug of the ocean on the millions of men who are suffering from the curse of CSB.

Men who suffer from CSB hardly ever leave the house in the hope of finding a home cure or an intervention, as we experts on the subject call it. There are some who leave home in search of a remedy and the side effects can lead to serious instability.

There are self-help remedies which do provide some temporary relief but the only worthwhile treatment involves active and interpersonal treatments. CSB – or chronic semen build-up – can be cured. The afflicted must find strategies for keeping the children busy during the treatment.

Barney was a great help back in the days of the video. Then

Peppa Pig was stuck in to the DVD player or the oldest plan of all was to buy the kids gallons of sweets.

Better still, get herself out of the house and make out in the car like ye used to do in the old days.

There should be CSB warnings in August, just like the pollen count bulletins given out on the news.

And the old advice is still best. Truly, in the context of CSB, prevention is better than the cure.

**THE ERROR WAS
COMPOUNDED WHEN
THE URINALS WERE RAISED
UP A COUPLE OF INCHES
TOO HIGH AND SMALL MEN
HAD TO JUMP UP TO PEE**

| 24 |

At Last, A Meeting Of The Waters And Victory In The Long Battle To Instal The Weeping Wall Of Listowel

March 23, 2012

LIKE most new things, it was shiny. I bent down on my knees to check if I could see my reflection. There in the sanctuary where water meets wind and no bird sings, I could see the sfumato outline of my worn face and an impressionist portrait of the greying curls that were once tensile and black.

For me this was the culmination of more than 20 years of tireless campaigning.

I watched the waters surge and gurgle. The babbling voice of the flow was a wonder to the ear. In the still of the very early morning, at about a quarter to noon, before the public would come to use our steel waterfall, the realisation came upon me that I had won a victory for men that would set me apart as a fearless campaigner, who never lost sight of his goal over the course of two decades.

I allowed myself the honour of christening this work of art. There was no point in coming here with a dribble. My kidneys hurt like hell and then I let go. The opening ceremony was a triumph. The receding gradient ensured no danger of any backwash, spillage or imperfect aim. You couldn't miss. It was like shooting elephants in a room, and for many years this place was the elephant in the room, but now at last I'd got the monkey off my back. I had made the first pee in the new stainless steel toilets of our pub.

The trouble started off 20 years ago, when we had to put in new urinals. The mother picked them out and I told her the urinals were too narrow and men with bad aims or a tendency to splay or spurt would either miss or splatter the wall or the floor.

"Don't you go telling me about how to run a bar," she said. "I'm here for 40 years and I've cleaned up my share of pee in my time."

"But you're not able to pee standing up," I said, "and surely me being a man, I know more than you about how men pee."

She got her way. The error was compounded when the urinals were raised up a couple of inches too high and small men had to jump up to pee.

So after this year's Writers' Week when the bank account was in good stead, I proposed we take out the old urinals and instal a new stainless steel wall. The mother was against it. She's the one who makes sure we don't go broke. The mother could run the EU for the week on Tuesday.

"The reasons are financial," she said. It would cost too much in bad times. Phil, who works with us and is the mother's close friend and adviser, agreed.

Said Phil: "There's nothing wrong with the old toilets that a bucket of water couldn't fix." Now, Phil is an intelligent and hard-working woman who is the backbone of our pub but I had to give it to her straight.

"Phil, you and the mother are going on and on about something ye know nothing about because neither of ye are men."

"Thank God," said the mother.

"What will we do with the old ones?" asked Phil, ever practical.

"We'll make holy water fonts out of 'em," I said, losing my patience now.

Larry, who could straighten out the Leaning Tower of Pisa with a tap of a hammer, backed me.

Larry was installing the weeping wall and told the tragic story of this small, peeing man jumping up and down like a pygmy, trying to find his way in the tall grass.

Now when Phil and the mother join forces, it would easier to break down the walls of the Aswan Dam with a water pistol.

"I'm at this business 60 years," said the mother, "and surely be to God after all my years, I know how men pee."

"She's right," added in Phil.

"But have ye you-know-whats?" I asked.

That quietened 'em and I went off and ordered the new toilet. The mother and Phil are still somewhat miffed, but they're coming round.

The Sam Maguire came on Saturday last and they put Kerry-coloured green and gold toilet blocks in the channel that takes the waters to the sewers.

I SUPPOSE I SHOULD
PUT UP WITH THE GRUMP.
MOST PEOPLE DODGE OFF UP
ONE OF THE MANY BACK WAYS
HERE IN LISTOWEL, WHEN
THEY SEE HIM COMING

| 25 |

Characters From A Small Town Who Manage To Make A Big Impression – The Grump

December 8, 2014

JOINED up two men into The Grump so no one around here would recognise him out of the paper.

It was done to protect the anonymity of the guilty.

The woman who hasn't had sex for 39 years says Paul O'Connell has a huge crush on her and he sends roses every day.

She didn't say how many, but I got the impression it was a quite a few, seeing as the overflow blooms had to be placed in a urine receptacle Mrs 39 stole from the hospital when she was in there lately for women's troubles.

Mrs 39 must have broken it off with Michael Bublé.

"I hate Fridays. Today is the day I hate the most." Mrs 39 folds her arms as she speaks because she imagines I'm always staring at her breasts.

"But," I said, "today is Saturday."

She took a step back so as to let me see she was properly angry.

"I never said it wasn't Saturday. I only said I hated Fridays."

But I know she's covering up. Every day is the same to her and she does the same things every day unless Paul or your man of the Bublés come calling.

I ask her why it is she doesn't like Fridays.

"Because I don't and that's why."

The journalist breaks out in me in spite of my best efforts and so I ask her again, although truth to tell I want to find out for me more than you.

"Tell me why you don't like Fridays? Ah go on."

I'm sorry now I asked. She's upset.

"Because my husband left me for another woman of a Friday and I hate fish."

This isn't a typo or a grammatical error. She always says "of a Friday" just like Mrs Do-Be, the women with the double-barrelled nickname, who is only one person.

Mrs Do-Be is a neighbour of Mrs 39 and she comes out with stuff like: "I do be always going to Mass of a Sunday" or "my husband does be mad for the bit of carry on when he do be drinking".

Some of you may not know what the bit of carry on means. It's a bit of the other thing.

By now you might have gathered that the women around these parts have no inhibitions when it comes to talking about sex, or the lack of thereof.

The Grump hates sex. "An overrated pastime," he calls it. He do be always cribbing about something.

"We'll pay for this fine November yet. Ballybunion beach will be down on top of us in no time at all, what with all the global warming."

The Grump doesn't like me very much, or even very little, so I try to avoid him.

Sometimes though he traps me when I'm just about to get out of the car and can't escape because The Grump blocks the door until he's finished giving out and telling me what I write should be wholesome.

He always says "in my day" as if he owned his day.

Here's a typical one out of him. "I hate the word gay. They kept to their own in my day. There's nothing gay about their carry on. It's downright unnatural."

So why don't I tell him, the Grump, all two of him, to go away and leave me alone? That's the convention of living in a small place. If you fall out with one person you could end up falling out with 20, such is the interconnection between all of us.

I try to tell him we're all God's kids, but he's at an age where there's no changing him and by arguing I only make him worse.

The Grump family are a decent enough bunch and the worst I've done to him is to clamber out the passenger door from the driver's seat on the pretext I was suffering from claustrophobia. That was the day he said I wasn't much of a writer, which he put down to the fact I had a very happy childhood.

I suppose I should put up with The Grump. Most people dodge off up one of the many back ways here in Listowel, when they see him coming.

The old people used to say "offer it up" and I do, for such is the fabric of small town life. Tolerance is as much to do with listening as anything else.

There's usually a reason why people are the way they are. One of the two who make up The Grump saw his Dad drop dead from a heart attack when the little Grump was only seven or eight. There's no excuse for the other lad in the hybrid. He too had a happy childhood

Mrs 39 tells me Paul O'Connell sent her daffodils "and not out of a bucket either." Paul must have gone to a pile of trouble and expense, what with the daffodils being ever so slightly out of season in late November.

Such is fervour. Michael Bublé sang 'Love me Tender' for her over the phone from Las Vegas and he has it very bad for Mrs 39.

While all this talk was going on, her little dog, who knows Mrs 39 better than anyone, was sitting on his haunches, looking up at his friend with very sad eyes.

It seems Mrs 39 has taken to setting the table for two and one of the neighbours tells me she talks to herself, out loud, quite a lot. It's loneliness, I think.

The kids hardly ever visit and her husband won't be coming back any time soon, seeing as he's long dead and in California at that.

You'd be just a little bit worried for Mrs 39.

But Paul is constant and "the boy of the Bublés" is trying his level best to get back with her for The Christmas.

CON WROTE LOVINGLY OF MEN BRINGING THE MILK TO THE CREAMERY BY DONKEY AND CART WEARING PARCELS FROM AMERICA OF ORANGE PANTS AND MULTI-COLOURED HAWAIIAN STYLE SHIRTS

26

In Memory Of A Genius Called Con Houlihan

August 21, 2012

THEY were poor but decent people, barely scraping a living on a small farm that was more water than land.

Con Houlihan's friends milked three cows and grew their own spuds and cabbage. Dried and salty bacon hung from the roof of their thatched cottage. The diet was simple. Bacon and cabbage for the dinner. Potatoes every day, and the odd feed of an old hen when her egg laying days were over.

There were no factories and the only employment to be had was in the shops of Castle Island or a maybe a few days hire with a bigger farmer. It may have seemed like an idyllic self- contained world of wholesome food and living off the fat of the land. In a way it was but the life of the small farmer was hard and money was always scarce.

Con idealised this world in his writing. He did not give the full picture. Con couldn't bring himself to tell the whole truth. These people were his friends and neighbours. How could he tell of the grinding poverty and embarrass his own ?

There was hardly a house in the hill country that didn't have several in the States or England. The money sent home afforded the occasional luxury and kept Ireland afloat. Con wrote lovingly of men bringing the milk to the creamery by donkey and cart wearing parcels from America of orange pants and multicoloured Hawaiian style shirts.

We have finally arrived, after a good few detours, at that neighbour's cottage in the highlands near the edge of the Houlihan's bog.

Con brought his own food. A loaf of his mother's home made

griddle bread, a drop of colouring for the tea in a Baby Power bottle, a couple of hard boiled eggs and maybe a lump of full- fat, home cured yellow bacon. His mother kept a small shop and Con brought a bag of penny sweets for the children.

In with him then to the neighbours, for the kettle was always boiling there over the turf fire, even in summer.

Con got a great welcome and he was asked to sit at the table while the woman of the house prepared a feast. Now Con knew these were poor people and you can imagine his surprise when five lamb chops with huge hoola hoops of fried onions and a haycock of pandy was placed before him.

There followed a dessert of jelly and custard. The red jelly was left in the huge saucepan it was set in. A full saucepan of custard was poured over the jelly. Con could hardly get off the sugan chair after the feed.

The Bean an Tí wet the tea but she couldn't bear to see such a big man, such a brainy man, and such a well-loved neighbour drinking the tea on its own. She put down another feed on the big, blackened cast iron griddle. A half pound of sausages, shop rashers and black pudding sizzled and whistled for Con. One of the clutch of children was sent out to search for a hen egg. He came back with two. One was fried and the other was boiled.

Con, being Con, ate every last bite. Out of politeness.

He told the whole story later that day at my Uncle Jim's shop. Con was so welcome there too. He was one of their own who went to university on scholarship, in times when only the rich could afford to go. Con graduated with first class honours from UCC. The people in an around Castle Island had a great love of learning and Con was declared a genius before he was no more than 20 years of age.

For all his brilliance young Con always spoke with a hand to his mouth. My mother put it down to shyness, "or maybe," she said, "it was his way of not showing off how brilliant he really was."

Con, it seems, might have had a crush on my Auntie Norrie but he was too shy to ask her out and there was the danger too he might spoil a lovely friendship.

My Uncle Jim told of how the poor family from the bog lands purchased vast quantities of groceries from his shop, so much so, the messages had to be brought up to the house in tea chests.

The family had the great good luck to get an inheritance from some far out cousin who died in America. There wasn't enough to live forever without working but the legacy was more than sufficient to provide a feed fit for Con Houlihan.

Some 60 years on my mother remembers every word of that story told in the country shop on the Road to Abbeyfeale and it was here too Con met my father for the first time.

John B cycled the 20 miles over the steep hills of Lyracrompane to see my mother. Con happened to be in the shop at the time and the young writers became friends for life, within minutes.

Con was already a rising star with regular pieces appearing in The Kerryman. He was also part of the editorial staff of two on the Taxpayers News, a radical paper set up in Castle Island by Charlie Lenihan. Charlie was a butcher and a farmer. He was one of the first to recognise Con's genius as a writer. The young Con not only produced articles on Sartre but also helped make Charlie's famous black puddings, which were exported to places as far away as Killarney and Tralee. Con maintained it was the printers ink from his mixing hand that gave the puddings an enduring darkness and unique flavour.

John B was young and eager. Con and John B had so much to talk about. Poems were said. Scraps of writing were read. Con praised Dad and gave him courage.

Dad walked his bike as far as Con's house, about two miles in towards Castle Island from Uncle Jim's shop. With the flow of the conversation, he missed the turn off for Listowel.

Con walked back with Dad from his own place to the edge of Lyre at a high place called the top of the Maam. The lights of Castle Island twinkled down below in the valley and the two talked of writing and of writers and of football and of rugby and of their dreams and fears, until the street lamps were turned off at dawn.

My grandfather Bill was a teacher and he was leaving for school when Dad arrived home to Church Street. "I was very worried John. Where in the name of God were you all night?" And the same man who was very mild-mannered was cross with my Dad. These were different times. No boyfriend would dare to stay out all night a courting back then.

"Ah," said my Dad to his Dad, "you'd never know who I met over in Mary's house, only Con Houlihan."

"That explains it all," said Granddad. "Sure wouldn't that man keep anyone out all night."

27

My Father – The 1952 Intermediate Final Hero

June 10, 2012

HE couldn't watch an all Ireland. Off with him then. Out to Dirrha bog, he walked at speed for the 70 minutes and prayed for Kerry until the rosary beads nearly fell off the chain from the constant erosion between his thumb and index finger.

My dad always knew the result of the match before he ever got back to the car. If Kerry were beaten, walkers would be out on the wetlands within minutes of the final whistle. They couldn't bear to watch another county lift Sam. Their forlorn faces and funereal gait told their own story.

If not a soul appeared in the bog, on would go the car radio and Mícheál Ó Muircheartaigh or Weeshie Fogarty or Liam Higgins would tell him that Kerry won.

Then he would watch the recording. And he'd watch it again every couple of days after that until the following May when the championship started and there were new games to be savoured.

His 10th anniversary was on Wednesday last. I'm not as sad as you might think. Not that I don't miss him. He was great sport.

It was about a fortnight before dad died that another John Keane passed away. John's sister Nora is married to Tadhg Moriarty and the Moriarty's are our friends and allies. Eugene Moriarty, who finished fourth in the world cycling championship, is one of the clan and is a true Corinthian.

Dad insisted on going to the graveyard. He was weak and very wobbly on his feet. On the way out he looked at me and said: "Sure it is hardly worth my while going home."

We broke down laughing even though both of us were fully

aware the ref was lifting the whistle to his mouth and that he would be back there for good, sooner rather than later.

We planted him in the left half forward position. There is no dice throw of pebbles over his grave. It's grass, like the small square in the football field over the wall.

On Monday night he will hear the shouts of players and spectators in the John B Keane League. He'll be sitting on the arch of a Celtic Cross, legs dangling as he looks out over the graveyard wall into Frank Sheehy Park. He'd be cheering on his granddaughter. In continuity there is a kind of here and now immortality.

Listowel Emmetts were always part of his life. His three sons played for the club. Conor and John made the Kerry minors and he was so proud, but he never let on in front of me.

On the night I was cut from Kerry minor training, he handed me a fiver and said: "Find a nice girl in Ballybunion and tell her your troubles."

He made no attempt to have me restored even though the trainer, Seamus MacGearailt was a good friend. Which is as it should be.

But he was always there to back you up when the going got tough. I was a senior at 16 and was propelled into orbit with a cowardly punch from an opportunist assassin who specialised in taking out young lads. Dad ran onto the pitch to save me.

I was mortified. Someone tried to hold him back but it would have been easier to mop up the Feale and squeeze it into a bucket. The bully bolted. He said he was more afraid of what my dad might say to him than any physical punishment.

I was about six and he was coming to the end of his career at 36. Some lad hit him a shoulder and down he went. I started to bawl crying and ran onto the pitch. And he was mortified. I'm told he was a very good player. Fast, if furious, with a great leap for the ball.

He was 70 and was recovering from several courses of

chemotherapy and radiation. Dad invited a young buck round the back of the stand in Listowel to sort things out. He was president of Listowel Emmets at the time and he felt he should avenge every insult to his beloved club.

He kissed me when I won all of my one North Kerry Championship back in the days when there wasn't much paternal kissing or hugging. Dad argued with half of Tarbert that day in the stands and 10 minutes after the match he was off drinking and singing with them.

That was him. The temper lasted no longer than a lightning flash but it was thunderous and spectacular.

He had a dark secret. Every family has one, but this is very, very bad. Couldn't be worse in fact.

My dad spent some of the happiest days of his life in Doneraile in County Cork, where he was a chemist's assistant.

Dad played for Cork in the national league game against Waterford. The game was abandoned when the pitch became flooded – with blood. The next round was against Kerry and he retired from Cork football before the game, undefeated.

Somewhere in the everywhere, he is with us. Exactly where he is, I do not know but I sense his presence. When I call to dad's allotment in the lea of the stands I feel he's advising me and I tell him my problems.

The days of rapid fire Hail Marys merging like a closing concertina have passed. Now I talk to him. Maybe I'm some sort of medium ventriloquist and it is me talking to me, but I'm pretty certain he is there in that somewhere over the rainbow.

Dad died at 6:27am on May 30th, 2002. On the 10th anniversary of his last act, I was up until nearly 3am getting ready for Writers' Week but I woke early. At 6:27am. And I didn't set my clock. I wouldn't mind but never once in his life did he call us for school.

When asked how he wanted to be remembered there was no mention of Oscars or doctorates. "I want to be known as the man who scored the winning point in the Kerry intermediate final of 1953."

Yes, I am happy we had him for so long and for the dad that he was. He was a great man for bringing small boys to big matches. It was Croke Park 1963 at the Grounds Tournament final between Kerry and Dublin. My first time. You never forget even if it was all those years ago. Dad lifted me up in his arms to show me the long drop from the height of the top of the Hogan stand.

"What if I fall, dad?"

"Don't worry Bill, boy," he said.

"You are safe here with me."

And I still am.

28

Meet The Man Who Has It All Figured Out

April 6, 2015

I KNOW a Man Who Has It All Figured Out. Don't even think about asking me who he is, and why he is the way he is, and how he figured it all out. Because I'm sworn to secrecy.

He's not from here and all I can say is the story comes from somewhere near you.

The play remains the same wherever you go in Ireland.

Only the actors change.

I'm probably guilty of being an accessory after the fact, as it is. And might end up doing time, if my defence of journalistic privilege doesn't hold up.

His wife is a seamstress and does a bit of invisible mending.

So invisible in fact, the tax man knows nothing at all about her little business.

He hasn't worked for years. Officially.

She's an old school wife. Peels his spuds, does the washing and irons his and other people's shirts. His for free.

She mowed the hankie lawn this morning, in honour of my visit.

The first mowing of the year left cuts on the fresh lawn like tank tracks.

A sure-footed cat trots across the orange front wall.

The house is unpainted and the cement front has turned a seasick green.

They pay a nominal rent for the house and have free or subsidised everything, from power to pills.

The Man Who Has It All Figured Out is very happy with his lot and has a higher disposable income than 83.76pc of the population.

"I'm never votin' for the feckers again," he says, with feeling.

"Go on," says I.

"Do you know what they done?"

"What did they do to you?"

"They went and med Viagra cheaper?"

I had better explain.

The patent ran out on Viagra and now it only costs a little, and as you all know a little goes a long way.

The Man Who Has It All Figured Out had a nice little sideline selling the Viagra he was getting for free, for €20 each, to a couple of customers who were too embarrassed to go into the doctor, or to the chemist.

"Not that I needed 'em myself," he adds.

He goes out for a smoke. The pack was bought from a man who dealt in cheap cigarettes which "fell off the back of a lorry".

The woman next door comes to the garden wall. They chat about the weather and the price of Easter eggs.

The Man Who Has It All Figured Out says goodbye with: "I'll be in later on to fix that for you."

There's a large ear on the gable wall bringing TV in through a dodgy box.

A black and white terrier with a clipped tail barks at me.

"Don't think I'm cooling her soup," he says.

"What?" says I.

"Herself next door," he says. "I just do little bits of odd jobs for the neighbours."

Another "little" earner.

We've just come back from a big dinner.

The Man Who Has It All Figured Out picked the restaurant. He knows his food from watching the cookery programmes on day-time TV.

He started with the prawns and when he said: "I've never had lobster before," I feared the worst.

"Maybe you could get it on the medical card?" I suggested.

He laughed it off and ordered the lobster anyway and an expensive bottle of wine from a place where the King of France kept a mistress or two.

I asked his wife to dinner, but he said she couldn't go because of the babysitting job she had on that evening.

More tax-free dosh.

She comes back in home. He goes out to read the paper for a neighbour who has poor sight.

And after he calls to the old lady two down who lives alone to make sure she has the fireguard on. He brings her the dinner every day, for free, and sits with her every night for a good while.

His wife is mad about him.

I tell her the story about the woman who complained about her husband.

"He eats my pension and he drinks his own."

She laughs.

"Is himself like that?" I ask

"Now that the boys are done for, he never asks me for money and he has a good heart.

"He never raises his voice and he only gave up work when the two boys left college."

"What are your boys at?"

"We thought they had it made when they went to university. They were nearly the first to go from around here but now they're in Australia."

She shows me the pictures.

"He told them to head off. There's nothing around here for you, he told them. He didn't want them to be scratchin' a livin' like us. Himself wanted them to go to a place where something would be thought of them."

Her husband was bitter. Lads with half his sons' abilities were in permanent jobs.

The couple are saving up to get enough money to go out to visit them.

"The house is very quiet without the boys," she says. "We're dying to see them."

The Man Who Has It All Figured Out came back in and I figured him out. He wants you all to figure it out for yourselves.

The Man Who Has It All Figured Out had another condition, other than anonymity. He asked me not to pass judgment on him.

"Just tell the story."

I did as I was asked. I'll leave the judging to you.

29

Looking For A Match At Lisdoon Leaves Dodgy Internet Dating For Dead

August 19, 2013

A SMALL man he was. Smaller than a jockey. He walked warily as if afraid of treading on a landmine. The jaw stuck out like a ledge and his cap hid his face. He wore an old suit. It could have been his confirmation outfit. The cuffs and collar of his clean white shirt were as frayed as if they had been scrubbed with a cheese grater. And it was as wrinkled as his weathered face.

The small man ordered a half-pint and called me 'Sir,' even though he was 30 years older.

My father passed in. He had this uncanny way of scanning the whole pub in seconds and figuring out exactly who everyone was, and why they were here.

"Do you see that little lad up at the counter? I know by the cut of him he's looking for a woman," he said.

And he was. Some smart boy in his native place took advantage of the small man and told him John B was a matchmaker. We were very nice to him, and my father advised the little man to try a few days in Lisdoonvarna, where the women were plentiful.

I'd like to report he married out of Lisdoon, but we never saw him again. The chances of his getting a woman were next to impossible. Why he left it so late, we will never know. Maybe if the man started in time he would still have failed. There weren't too many who would fit, and he was choosy. "What do you think of your one sitting over there?" I asked.

"She's not too bad," he replied, "but she has a button missing in her cardigan."

I walked him to the bus.

"What do you think of my chances?" he asked.

"You'd never know," I lied.

"I'm not too badly off," he said. "Sure, haven't I the television for the bit of company and the neighbours are very good to me. I never ates the Christmas dinner alone."

There were very few matchmakers left in Ireland around the time the little man in search of love called to see us. It was in the 1980s, and matchmaking was regarded as hilarious or barbaric, depending on your take.

There were no mobile phones or emails. I have little doubt but that many of you reading this would be married or partnered to someone else if there were mobiles, Facebook or Twitter back then. We didn't even have a proper landline system. Most phone boxes were vandalised or stinking of urine, and you'd never know who'd be listening in.

Dating or matchmaking websites have taken over from the old-style matchmakers. This has to be good. It's not easy to meet someone when you hit a certain age. Especially for women. Men find it easier to drift in and out of bars, but many women are too shy to go into a pub on their own. I would encourage women to be brave. If someone passes a remark or gives you "the look", it says more about them than you.

There are so many fine people in search of love. Older and younger. There's nothing to be ashamed of. Go on line. Somewhere back in your ancestral past there was a match. There's the very real possibility your grandparents were matched up.

Most of us want to love and be loved. It is the strongest of desires and needs. But there is a lack of respect for basic human dignity in many of the matchmaking websites. Last week, BBC's 'Panorama' exposed the shocking exploitation of vulnerable people. False identities were set up by unscrupulous dating agencies who boosted traffic on their sites by pretending to be genuine people in search of partners. The victims were interviewed, and you could feel their hurt and humiliation.

Those in search of the most fundamental of human rights are being used and abused.

Usually what happens in the States hits here about five years later. Good and bad. It is our opinion that in the next few years most couples who are matched up will get together through the internet.

The internet is either a weed or a flower, depending on your take. Child pornography has been rightly targeted as a subject for intervention and control, but experience has shown the major players see their corporations as some sort of super-national entity beyond the reach of sovereign states.

We cannot trust the big internet dating companies to self-police in any meaningful way. Accountability often only comes when they are forced into reform. Even in the case of child pornography.

It has been said the net is too big to police, but if there was billions to be made out of some new technological invention, then for sure a way to track down the abusers would probably be found.

Alan Shatter, our Justice Minster, should prepare a position paper on internet dating. Ireland can lead the way. Most politicians do not plan. They react. Now is the time to make preparation for the future and present developments in the way we choose our mates.

Topics for discussion must include security, privacy, the prevention of fraud and guidelines as to the monitoring of sites by state agencies. Legislation should be prepared allowing investigators to audit the activities of the dating sites with appropriate sanctions for hosts and users.

But the old ways are best. Next week sees the start of the Lisdoonvarna Matchmaking Festival. There's dancing all day and all night. Chatting up and spontaneity. Go to Lisdoon or anywhere where destinies collide and sample the hard copy. And if the old boy who called to us all those years ago is still to the good, please try to fix him up with your friend.

THE WALK IS ONE
OF SOFT TALK AND
WHISPERS. OF LOVE
AND MEMORIES.
THERE'S A HEALING HERE
AND A HELPING TOO

30

If You Make The Walk From Darkness Into Light, You Will Never Walk Alone Again

May 4, 2015

DARKNESS into Light brings us on a spiritual journey of hope and remembrance. We will join those who went before us as we remember loved ones who surely walk with us.

The gathering in Listowel, Kerry, on Saturday is a coming together of bodies and souls. The community of friends will meet up at the Parade Ring in Listowel racecourse.

We will start out in the darkest of the night, as we walk all along the banks of the silver River Feale.

The friends will cross the Island Bridge and continue on our journey past the towers of the 13th century Desmond Castle and into the town square of dreaming spires and elegant lines.

On with us, then, down to the old oak woods of the Cow's Lawn, where writers walked to clear the head and begin new imaginings.

Friends who have lost loved ones will light the way with little yellow night lights of remembrance. The walk is one of soft talk and whispers. Of love and memories. There's a healing here and a helping too. From the dark of the night woods, we take to the quiet, still streets of the heritage town of Listowel, where the candles in every window will light our way.

Back then with us, over the Greenville Bridge to the racecourse, where we all started out, for tea and talk. The two bridges have been crossed. The circle is complete and unbroken. We welcome in the dawn's first rays on this day of love, hope and renewal.

Some 80,000 people will walk for Pieta House all over Ireland and in Sydney and New York.

It's the first year in New York. Our emigrants are often lonely and without the security of the green card or citizenship. There will be a Pieta House opening in New York very soon and the plan is to extend the Pieta care to several more cities in the States. There's a walk in Killarney, where thousands will show their faith in the cause and in Dingle too, where the good people of the west are hosting their first Darkness into Light event.

Pieta was founded by Joan Freeman when she lost a loved one. Joan took a step back as chief executive last year and now she is an ambassador who travels Ireland and beyond as part of her mission to help out. We are old friends. Joan loves people and she's a born communicator. There's a grace about her and the feeling that she knows our frailties but loves us all just as much. Some civilizations and religions believe the eyes mirror the soul. More claim the eyes are the gateways to the soul.

Joan has empathy in her eyes.

Cora O'Brien is our Listowel leader. She rules in a very easygoing way but the job gets done. There's a template there for many big companies who seem to think that just short of bullying brings the best results out of their employees.

Cora has the moral authority, you see. For our Cora lost her 16-year-old David to suicide. I knew him well and he was a lovely lad. Cora's husband, Martin, gets stuck in too and he helped in no small way with the setting up of the New York walk.

Martin and Cora turned their worst day in to some of the best. They had their own Darkness into Light journey. They got all of us together and a few years ago, on a cracked June evening, we broke the world record for the most people dressed as nuns with all the money raised going to Pieta.

And yes, it is true. I gave an old GAA cup as the first prize for the best Nunderwear. You can register online and we will be in MacAuliffe's Gift shop from Monday to Friday, here in Church Street, in Listowel.

We will pass the old graveyard and candles on the wall will keep the departed on our side. The walk goes by a place where a boy died by suicide. I always say a prayer for him on my walks, and hope he will find some comfort from our passing by the place where his life ended so tragically. I believe that by walking as one, we somehow ease the pain of those who died by suicide and that the spirits of the lost ones rest easier. I have no proof. It's just what I believe and that belief is the only way I can make sense of the taking of precious lives. The lost become found and the coming together of all of us gives great comfort. Our walk then, is a journey of the spirit and the spirits walk beside us.

The aching I'm feeling this morning for a friend I lost many years ago is tough to handle. I often feel I could have done more back then. I should have seen the signs, but I didn't. I should have been less caught up in my own troubles. I should have taken just a few seconds to tell him he was the most caring and kindest of people. Sometimes, that's all it takes.

I wish the me now, even with all my imperfections, could have been there for my friend back then. The only way I can ease the pain is by walking on Pieta night and by passing on my story to you in the hope you might spread the kind word. So many suffer from a suicide. The fallout is nuclear for family and friends.

I must stress the column is just a personal view. I have no training in all this, but Pieta does. Pieta has opened up in Tralee just recently and there are Pietas all over the country. The Kerry Pieta home is in Moyderwell and there is no more welcoming place. Joan has always seen Pieta as a home. An open house where our friends feel free to open up. Pieta is easy to access. The counselling is free and you will be seen in a few days.

The counsellors are trained and Pieta has years of experience in dealing with self-harm and those who are suicidal. They will help you get better. There's a cure there for sure. And no one judges.

Pieta is a place of candles and sofas and flowers, with tea, biscuits and much love. You will be made so welcome and as we often say here, if the good times didn't last forever, then neither will the bad. This too shall pass. And if you walk with us, from the Darkness into Light, never again will you walk alone. Love and hope are only a step away.

dil.pieta.ie

31

Keeping Pub Doors Open Can Really Be A Burden – But The Fun Makes Up For It

September 23, 2013

'M like a Tayto bag that gets blown up and then burst. It's the Sunday after the Listowel Races. The Sunday after optimism. It was a few years back when I met him. The old boy. He was worn out after race week. His face was as yellow as a newspaper left out in the sun. Thin, swollen veins crisscrossed his cheeks. The old boy was fond of drink and late nights. The drink made him forget he wasn't a young buck anymore. He partied until dawn and now he trudged down to work. Men have walked faster down death row.

Reality hit. Problems postponed mounted up before him. Unopened bills with harps on the front played a sad melody. Ah but it was all so different a week ago. The big wheel was spinning in Bird's funfair. He chanced it and went back up for a second go. The lorry carrying the big wheel pieces out of town moved slowly too.

I knew how he felt, that old man. When I was a boy I wanted a job as the hero who jumped up on the back of the bumpers to help out pretty girls who were getting bumped too much by young lads. Crashing into girls in the bumpers was a courting ritual around here that still continues. Strange but true. The dodgem rodeo riders could cross the track by jumping from car to car without ever touching the ground. Saving girls.

The old boy was trying to put the key in the front door but he kept missing. His little terrier looked up at him with all the pity in the world. Pets take moods from their owners. The dog's face was as sad as an orphan nobody wants to take home from the pound.

Mr Thing who is always in good form whenever everyone else is depressed praises himself for speaking his mind.

"Ye're paying for the high life now," he says to the old boy and me.

"Cheer up," he says as he twists the dagger to make sure it causes maximum damage to the internals. "It's only 358 days to next year's races. Ha ha ha," he goes. But he speaks the ha ha ha 'cos it would kill him to laugh.

We try a drop of coffee. He says it gives him heartburn. He uses the spoon to heap up a dose of bread soda and he eats it in one go. Bread soda is an old cure for indigestion.

My friend gathers his thoughts into some bit of coherence.

"Tell you the truth, Billy," he replies, "either a good ride or a bad dinner would finish me off."

I get the paper. All bad news.

The little dog follows me up the street. He confirms the limits of his jurisdiction by urinating against the pole that says Ballybunion nine miles. I go back for the duvet. And try to pretend it's next year.

But this year I was good. No drink. I'll bound into the bank tomorrow morning. Monday to you. Ah but I'll be the cocky boy.

The lads who come into the bar come out with stuff like; "You'll need a wheelbarrow to bring it down to the bank," or "you must be ballin' dem fifties."

The illusion of having money is short-lived. It took me some time to discover there's a subtle difference between turnover and profit. There are so many bills to catch up on but at least they get paid on the Monday after the races and that gnawing worry goes for a while anyway.

I feel a special responsibility to keep up the tradition. Dad came home from England with his savings. He worked at a dangerous furnace in Northampton. My Mam was a hairdresser in Castle Island. Between them they put together the deposit to buy John B's. That was 58 year ago and we're still in business.

Like most of you in small pubs we struggle at times but the races and Writers Week give us a massive lift.

We get the same people back year after year. Customers become friends. Then you hear the news that a friend who has been coming to the races for 20 or 30 years has passed away or is ill. There's no time to be sad at the races. Too busy we are. Sadness and worries are put on hold until the day after. But we missed Colm Murray so much this year.

Sometimes I find the responsibility of keeping the doors open to be a very heavy burden but the fun more than makes up for the worry days. We had 30,000-plus at the races on Ladies Day. The beauty and style were a joy.

This other oul lad in the bar was admiring a beautiful girl wearing a very short skirt. "Billy," he said, "it's like barbed wire. Enough to protect the property but not too much to obscure the view."

The races will keep the cheques from bouncing and the standing orders from sitting down.

The man who speaks his mind was upset on the Tuesday after this year's Writers Week. He was in a long queue in the bank. I was lodging a big bundle of money into the new machine. There were only a couple in front of me.

"Fine for some," said the man who speaks his mind, "the big shots don't have to go queueing away up like the rest of us. So they don't."

"Ah," I said to him, "the new machine is only for people with two million or more in the bank."

This time he was the one heading for the duvet. I'll avoid him all today. He'll be far too cheerful for the day after the races.

I HAVE WATCHED YOU BOTH
DO THE SIMPLE THINGS WELL.
CONTINUE AT THAT.
LIFELONG COMMITMENT IS A
THRESHOLD. A MARRIAGE IS
NOT A BUSINESS RISK

32

Wise Words About Love – From A Man Who Has Never Walked Down The Aisle

January 11, 2016

THE priest stopped half way through the wedding Mass as if the irony of it all had hit him just then for the first time. "Isn't it strange", he said, "that a man who was never married is telling all of you how it should be done."

And he got a fit of laughing. So too did everyone else in the church – but there was hardly anyone there in St Mary's who agreed with him.

For all of us present were very much in agreement that the singleton, Fr Pat Moore, had just delivered a masterclass on marriage.

We go back a while. Pat was in my class in St Michael's here in Listowel before he was spirited away to St Brendan's in Killarney, which at that time was a kind of a prep school for would-be priests. We have written here before about Moore, as we used to call him in school. Pat has been through a fierce battle against cancer. He had a good bit of his body cut away just a few months ago. He only barely survived.

His friend and protégé Ger Barret and his lovely bride Grainne O'Sullivan were getting married and Pat had to be there.

Ger, still in his twenties, is a renowned filmmaker. His low-budget movies 'Pilgrim Hill' and 'Glassland' are little masterpieces. Keep an eye out for him. This lad is the real deal.

We all met up the night before the wedding for a drink. Moore was still shaky on his feet, like a newborn calf, but he's on the mend and getting stronger by the day. He knows me better than most:

"Make sure you're on time for the wedding," he said.

I was there for the throw-in.

You couldn't refuse Moore anything. I knew from the tone of his voice and the dancing in his eyes that this was going to be worthwhile.

Ger and Grainne come from Bedford and Carrueragh in north Kerry and they are soulmates. Grainne is a solicitor.

She is the practical one who keeps a close eye on Ger's projects. Ger is a dreamer who makes his dreams a reality.

I knew from the very beginning that Ger would make the grade. He has a wisdom beyond his years and everything he sees around him is stored, processed and then framed with so much compassion and great skill.

Here is some of Fr Pat's sermon delivered just a week ago. But this is more than a sermon. It is a love template for the ages: "None of us comes to a relationship with empty hands. We are all formed in homes, whether in Bedford or Carrueragh. We carry in the blood or in the mind the images of those who have loved us and whom we have loved. We carry damage, too, wherever we are wounded.

"These images we have carried for years, they are set in the mind, they are the lenses through which we view things. So often we can't see through the net of these patterns. The magic of love is what Grainne and Ger have. It releases an energy.

"New thresholds have opened up. And the grace of new beginnings. Life quickens with new possibilities, fresh invitations, when a couple sense the complexity and delight of it all."

Fr Pat stops for a while to give us a chance to take it all in.

The priest asks us to cross over through the centre aisle to shake hands with the guests. It's a part of him, that desire to connect everyone up. Then, when the greetings are done, my old school pal continues with his conversation.

"Love," says Father Pat, "is a great shelter within which vulnerability can be shown and gradually healed. Awakening and growth of love can be fascinating to watch. It arrives from nowhere. It calls two strangers from the crowd. They become a shelter to each other."

I'm thinking now of my friend as I pass on his words of love and I sense a sadness. Because of his calling, Moore missed out on the intimacy of a relationship. But in another way his sacrifice has brought him into all of our lives.

The priest's loneliness must be hard to bear at times, but this man who gives out all he has in his heart with such humour and tact will never be short of love.

We will go back to the sermon. Well, it's not really a sermon – more of a sharing, I would call it. Back to Moore, then.

"To love somebody is an art. It doesn't come simply or cheaply, it is a lifetime's work. It is a risk. There will be storms, but there will be times when the beauty of your lives together brings unexpected joy. Deeply buried hurts will resolve and release themselves.

"Healing light flows from unknown regions of the heart.

"Love does change everything. Where there is fear, courage begins to dawn, confusion gives way to clarity. In old walls unexpected doors open. Hearts awaken.

"Here is St Mary's Church, in this house of wise and intuitive shelter, God's house, you are surrounded by family, friends, people who wish you well."

This is me again. He's tired now. The cancer has taken its toll.

There's a silence while he catches his breath. But the priest carries on. He looks over to Ger and Grainne: "I have watched you both do the simple things well. Continue at that. Lifelong commitment is a threshold. A marriage is not a business risk.

"Every day our lives are braided with luminous moments. Sometimes the most fleeting moments reveal themselves to be the things of greatest substance. You both do sense that – continue to do so."

There it ended with a smile, and he married the happy couple. Now I know why Moore told me to get to the church in time.

His words were universal and true. There was a grace there in the old church.

Those moments illuminated the grey January day – and the man who never married lit up all of our lives with his harvest of lifelong wisdom.

| 33 |

Ultrasound Picture Shows A Tiny Baby, Not A Foetus Or An Embryo Or A Thing

July 22, 2013

I HAVE been putting off writing this column for weeks now. I was afraid. It is not easy for a man who writes about women's issues. Not easy to play God either.

I am for gay marriage, contraception, women priests, sex between consenting adults, a free press and equal rights for all.

Most of my friends are in the liberal camp. I often have difficulty here in expressing forthright views because of cowardice, the wish to be seen as everyone's friend and also because I have so many skeletons rattling around in my cupboard that there is hardly room to store a tin of beans. There is a very slippery slope attached to the high moral ground.

The baby in the womb is a baby, not a foetus or an embryo or a thing. The idea that a baby is not a baby makes no sense either morally or medically. How is it that, say in England, a baby's life cannot be ended from 24 weeks on but at 23 weeks, 23 hours, 59 minutes and 59 seconds it can be destroyed? Euphemisms should not be applied to life and death in the womb.

Any one of you who has seen a baby swimming happily in the placenta pool, all hands and legs like an astronaut marionetted by gravity in a spaceship, will probably agree that the ultrasound scan on the screen is the most beautiful movie ever made. For me this was the clinching argument.

I have friends who have had terminations. Decent women who saw no way out. This sounds like a corny line from a bad country song, but it is not easy being a woman.

Please do not categorise me with the extremists who not only cast the first stone but the second too and many more as well. Or with those who have picketed politician's private residences, where their wife and kids live.

I abhor the stance of those so-called Christians who have no empathy for women in a dreadful predicament not of their making.

I feel that if a woman is raped she should be allowed a termination. There is still going to be a death. But if the girl who has been violated stands little chance of recovering from her ordeal without a termination, then it should be her choice. If the mother's life is in danger, then it is the mother's call whether to have a termination or not. Whatever choice she makes is the right one. Jesus himself bleeds for women who have to make such decisions.

But the truth, as I see it, is that the baby in the womb is the underdog. Who is going to protect the little baby? That is what bothers me so much. Who is going to speak up for the boy or girl with no voice?

I have a feeling there are many more men who feel the same way but are unable to properly develop their feelings because of our shared guilt at the way women have been mistreated by men over the years in this country. We feel unworthy.

Last year, 32 girls under 16 travelled to the UK for abortions. Do you think I am going to condemn these kids or their parents? More than likely there is a kid on the plane this morning. Her mammy is probably sitting beside her, holding her hand. Her daughter is scared. Most likely confused. Probably she has been swayed by the adults in her life. Maybe she is suicidal. She is only a kid. Man, but you would wonder how it is that whichever almighty you worship allows such suffering and torture in the world. The baby inside the little girl will not be coming back to Ireland. The little girl will return and her life will be changed for ever. Suffer little children. Mother and child.

All we can do is say a few Hail Marys to the best mother of all.

Maybe more can be done here on Earth. Sex education is the

key to stopping teenage terminations. We must be honest and open with teenagers. A mental health professional told me most teenagers do not have a clue about contraception, and most teenagers are having sex.

There are no easy answers. The newly passed abortion bill will lead to abortions in Ireland. But very few. The politicians found the easiest way out.

The status quo will remain in practice. No mother will allow her 14-year-old daughter to go before three doctors. It is a lot easier to book a cheap flight to England and present at a clinic where no one knows you. There are no degrees of separation in this country. As usual, only the poor and the most vulnerable will suffer most. Their pro-choice is no choice. The poor will take the option of appearing before three doctors who will decide whether or not the mother is suicidal. But most will somehow find the money for England.

Every now and then, life being what it is, unsolvable cases will come before the courts.

What about the father who does not want to see his child's life terminated? Yes, it is the woman's body that will be invaded. The woman will bear the bulk of the post- and pre-stress of what will be the most traumatic moments of her life, but men have rights too. We are not just some sort of anonymous donors who make deposits at a sperm bank. But it is the woman who will lose out, always, whatever choice she makes.

We are out of our depth. I am, for sure. A terrifying range of conflicting emotions swirl around in the brain. You want the best for the mother. You want the best for the baby. Sometimes the two wants conflict. This is work for God, not man.

**YES, THE PROPERTY TAX
IS HIGHER IN CITIES BUT
THE WORST PROPERTY TAX
OF ALL IS THREE YEARS
OF BAD WEATHER**

34

Hardly A Tear Shed For Honest Farmers As Crisis Pushes Many Over The Edge

May 20, 2013

THE worst part is they are not even angry. There are no marches or rants from fiery demagogues in strong country accents or tractor blockades or stormings of Ministers' offices. And there's hardly a word about the worst farming crisis in living memory.

Yesterday I looked in vain for any mention of the fodder crisis. Maybe a statement from the Minister as to a big cash injection for our farmers, who are as near to broken as they have been at any time since calves were sent floating down the river in their thousands back in the time of the economic war with England.

Mother earth of the farming heartland is cold and drowned.The grass sits up like the spikes on a hedgehog's back. Where there is some growth, the fields are too wet to travel with heavy machinery needed for cutting silage. Cattle are starving and farmers and farm families are in the dykes of despair.

Yet if a couple of hundred people were sold dodgy apartments in our capital city or a couple of hundred more were flooded out of their homes, there would be a massive outcry with intensive news coverage. We do not begrudge these people who have also suffered their share and more, but the numbers are very small in comparison to the scale of the farm crisis. It's a lot easier to cover a story in Ballsbridge or Leeson Street than a far away townland in West Cork or North Donegal.

And yes the property tax is higher in cities but the worst property tax of all is three years of bad weather.

But maybe there's a tendency to say this is just another case of crying wolf. Farmers are notorious for the poor mouth. That's not the case this time out. Listowel based vet Sean Treacy told of the scale of the disaster. "Four of my clients have gone out of business in the last few weeks and it's getting worse. The cattle are depressed. It's a form of bovine SAD. The cattle have been indoors since last August or even earlier in some cases. They are in poor shape physically and mentally. It's very sad to see."

"Farmers," he says, "would rather starve than see their cattle hungry."

It's a generational thing. Their ancestors built up the herd over 50 or 60 years. We cry when we lose a much loved dog we have had for 10 years. Can you imagine the poor farmers who have to see decades of breeding sold off with no more of a requiem than the bang of a gavel on an auctioneers table.

I couldn't get anyone to give a name to tag the words. I think some farmers might be in some way ashamed they are not able to carry on. That their link is the one that has broken the chain going back hundreds of years. They should not blame themselves. The odds were attacked against these brave men and women who worked so hard to keep afloat in the deluge. How is it that during our worst ever recession the weather has turned against us?

When I was a boy and the sun shone, I remember a few farmers discussing the case of a reckless dairy man who went to Spain for a week's holidays. "They'll have his place up on the pole before long," said one man. Meaning the holidaymakers farm would be put up for sale. These men's holidays were one day in Ballybunion, for the Pattern, on the 15th of August. They would roll up their trousers to the shins. Dip their toes in the surf and quickly withdraw as if was a bath of acid. The annual holy day holiday was over all too quickly and it was a rush back home for the five o'clock milking by hand.

On another occasion I brought a cousin to the beautifully manicured Ballybunion Golf Club for a bite of lunch. To show the place off to him. He just didn't get it. The idea of "all that land lying idle". A good farm spoiled.

The farmers love their land and they love their animals but you'd often wonder if the handing over of a family farm, especially a small farm , is more of a burden than a blessing. A property tax.

The banks will not lend any money to distressed farmers. The numbers do not add up. The cost of a big bale of imported hay is around €145. One bale will last a herd of 60 cows just one day. That's if you can get a bale. This morning there were queues outside Listowel creamery for the few bales that were available from Kerry Co- Op who are selling the hay at cost price. It was sad to see. Proud men all. In line. Men who worked hard all their lives. Waiting for relief. For four hours. In front of the whole world. Some of them had to go home empty-handed.

My friend cried when I called to him yesterday morning. He is small farmer who manages to keep going. Just about. One of the last of the smallholders. They are decent honest people, who only ever borrowed what they could pay back. When the farmer has a few shillings to spare, we all gain here in our little town. Contrary to the myth, farmers do spend money. The small towns will go soon if this keeps on. Is ar scáth a chéile a mhaireann na daoine. People depend on each other. The cities will suffer too. My mother told me of the day she went shopping with two farmers' wives in Dublin.

It was the first time ever they had 'folding money', back when Mark Clinton was Minister and the EU subsidies started to roll in. One of the farmer's wives bought a coat in Brown Thomas. My mother overheard the shop lady say: "Oh how I wish I married a farmer."

I'm not sure if there's too many takers now.

The last time I saw the small farmer cry was at his mother's grave.

The cattle were skinny. Their plaintive lowing echoed out from the milking parlour across the farm yard. "They have nottin to do all day only stand around," he said.

He'll soon be in the same state himself.

In the short term, the stakeholders must loosen the purses. This tragedy must not happen, ever again. We have a national plan for snowy weather but none for wet weather. The co-ops, the farming PLC's, the government, the banks, the EU and the farming organisations must act as one. Make a plan or farming as we know it now will be finished in this country. A few big ranchers will own all the land. The banks will look after them alright and there will be economies of scale to suit big business after the clearances.

But there's hope. "Farmers are a resilient bunch," says Sean Treacy. "The farmers are so used to ordinary disasters that they see this is as just a terrible disaster. A couple of fine days and they will be upbeat again. Their nature is to fight on and stay positive."

The priests prayed for fine weather at mass today and as you look out the window this Monday morning, the skies should be blue as the mercury crawls slowly up the tube. Long may it stay that way.

They're tough, the farmers, but one or two more bad years and even the bravest, the luckiest and the holiest will have to sell up.

35

Communion Day – When Grown-ups Can Reclaim Lost Or Forgotten Values

May 13, 2013

THE children are bouncing up from the church now. There's timelessness in the pageant. The big, bad world has pruned childhood years, yet the innocence of the little girls in their white dresses, white shoes and white lace veils is a constant. The boys look as boys should, in their school uniforms with ties slung to one side, shirts stuck out in little triangles and buttons tied out of sequence, pushing one collar above the other. Every day should be Communion Day.

I went door-to-door in my shiny short pants, white shirt and red tie, collecting. Out hustling the neighbours, like a little beggar child. Stuck to my jacket was the red and white rosette of the Virgin Mary, St Joseph and the Baby Jesus, all sitting on the donkey with shins as thin as drinking straws. The badge was Holy Communion accreditation. Before long the collection grew into a tidy sum. As much as a working man would earn in a fortnight.

My father got on well with nearly all the neighbours but there was one man he couldn't abide. They fell out years before over football and politics. My father's enemy was delighted to see me, he said. The enemy gave me half a crown. "And make sure to tell your father I was asking for him."

I threw the money up on the counter of our family pub, like a proud cowboy showing off his wages after a long cattle drive.

My father was mortified. Martin Luther was still a Catholic but I remember the day as if it was now. I kicked up. It wasn't the money. It was the bragging rights. The big question in class the next day was "how much did you make?"

Nowadays, the teachers tell the kids to keep the amount quiet, so as not to embarrass the children whose purses and pockets are light or empty. My father would laugh it off with most of the neighbours but years later he told me of the visit to the man he didn't like.

"I never thought things were so bad," he said to my father, insincerely, in a pitying voice that was intended to wound. "Ah, but I suppose Johneen, the oul' pub is going bad and there's no wan readin' that oul' shite you're writing."

The father was livid but he took a bullet for his seven-year-old. He knew if he answered back, the story would gather millipede legs.

The church has upped the receiving age by a year and now the children probably have a better understanding. But it is still the age of innocence.

A priest friend told me he often gets as many as five or six silent confessions. The kids just can't remember any sins. Which is lovely.

Indeed, the custom now is for the children to go up to the altar and whisper no more than four sins into the priest's ear. Only the words used now are "hurting God" and there's no mention of Hell or Purgatory, which was a kind of half-way house between Heaven and Hades. After the begging expedition, I was certain I was for a long incarceration in Purgatory. Maybe being a bar man is a type of Purgatory here on earth.

But the church has changed for the better. In some respects, anyway. Communion Day has become child-centred.

A teacher told us of the tearful seven-year-old who ran up to her and said: "Miss, I'm very upset, I was away the day you were givin' out the sins."

And there's the one about one of the neighbour's kids who told me his four sins. "Cursin', fightin', kickin' and spittin'."

Fr Pat Moore, parish priest of Duagh, tells of his own First Communion and the way the sun shone on the gold of the tabernacle and how he knew there was something wonderful inside.

It's an image that stayed with Pat and, eventually, when he became a priest he got his hands on the keys of the tabernacle. Pat sees the day as an opportunity for the grown-ups to reclaim lost or forgotten values.

The American writer Pearl S Buck wrote: "Every great mistake has a half-way moment, a split second when it can be recalled and perhaps remedied."

There are days when I think back on some of the decisions I made that have caused so much hurt. I struggle to forgive myself at times because I know now that in hindsight there was a half-way moment when I could have stopped.

The recollection of the days of innocence and the resurrection of lost childhood values are there to be taken from the First Holy Communion experience.

Knowing right from wrong was easy then, and it still is. If you're not sure, just go back to the little boy or girl you once were before the leery ways of the wicked old world led you astray and stole away your innocence on the rocky road to perdition.

"It's never too late to be what you might have been," wrote George Elliot and so there is a message of hope in the sacraments of confession and communion. It's there for all of us, irrespective of creed or no creed. You will find the answers to most questions of morality in the long-ago of childhood.

All we have to do is open the door of the gold tabernacle.

THE RUMOURS ARE THAT DONALD WILL BAN ALL TIPPERARY PEOPLE FROM ENTERING CLARE. THE BRIDGE BETWEEN BALLINA AND KILLALOE WILL BE COVERED WITH BARBED WIRE

36

If Trump Doesn't Win Over There – Beware His Plans For Clare

December 14, 2015

AND the worst part of it all is that if Donald Trump fails to win the Republican nomination, well then his next target will be Ireland. We have an exclusive here for you: The Donald wants to become The Taoiseach, and he has chosen a tried and tested route.

We will get back to the Irish angle soon enough and the possible banning of Tipperary people from entry into a certain neighbouring county over a narrow border bridge.

I was trying for ages and ages to think up a one-word description of Donald. 'Bigot' came to mind, as did 'warmonger'. 'Megalomaniac' was a definite. And in a kinder moment, even the word 'entrepreneur' was a possibility. After all, the man has built very high buildings, usually called after himself, and he is very wealthy. 'Demagogue' is my favourite though at the moment.

A demagogue plays to the worst vices and prejudices of the vulgar mob and tells them what they want to hear.

To tell the truth, I couldn't have cared much about him or what he got up to until he proposed a ban on all Muslims entering the US.

Hitler wasn't getting anywhere much with his political career until he picked on the Jews and blamed them for all the troubles of the world.

Now I'm not suggesting for a minute that Donald is intent on slaughtering all Muslims in death camps, but you would be sort of just a big bit uneasy about the man having access to the red button on the nuclear PlayStation.

He's going well in the polls in America. I'd say he thinks everyone loves him, even the Muslims. Donald says the Muslims told him: "Donald, you brought something up to the fore that is so brilliant and so fantastic."

He didn't actually mention the Muslims' names.

I suppose we better give him his say. When asked if was upset about being compared to Hitler, who proposed a ban on all Jews in Germany, Donald replied: "If that were true, it would bother me tremendously. But of course if you were a racist you probably wouldn't care. But if things are true, it would bother me. But if it's so false, and honestly I don't hear it often."

Ah really. Go on. Donald, it seems, ducks reality at every opportunity.

There's a difference though. Hitler banned the Jews from leaving Germany. Donald will not let the Muslims into the United States.

So the Muslim son goes to visit his father who is sick in England but he's not allowed back into the US. That sort of thing is just one of the many human rights abuses Donald will visit on the Muslims who love him so much.

Here's what I think happened. Donald is always getting big, huge ideas like the building of a hotel here or knocking one down there. That sort of thing. So he talks the ideas out without thinking and then at some meeting the ideas are evaluated by his staff and the mad ones are kicked out. But there was no filter for his travel ban on Muslims.

Now the mad plan has turned on Donald. There are moves to have him banned from entering Great Britain. You can be sure that the next time Donald arrives in Ireland he will not be met by ministers and colleens playing harps. Indeed, we have anti-discrimination laws – and banning people on religious grounds would be a breach of our laws.

Donald bought the Doonbeg Golf Resort in Co Clare. Are Muslims welcome? I have been to the village of Doonbeg and there's no more friendly place anywhere.

But do they know of Donald's masterplan?

It was back in 1917 and us Irish were doing our very best to free Ireland from British rule. Éamon De Valera, who was to become our future leader, was nominated to run for the British House of Parliament, in Co Clare of all places.

De Valera had a resounding victory and his big win in Clare was the beginning of a hugely successful political career.

He went on to become Taoiseach and ruled Ireland as a fundamentalist and conservative leader for many years.

So Donald, who knows his history, sees this hotel and golf course for sale in Clare and he decides to buy it up. Everyone here is thrilled because there will be a large investment and jobs.

So far so good. But we know Donald's real plan. He wants to acquire Ireland. And just like De Valera, he will put his name forward as a candidate in the forthcoming general election.

Today a hotel, tomorrow a country, and as Donald very much likes calling his acquisitions after himself, his people could rebrand Ireland as Trumpland.

The ancient sport of hurling gets hot and heavy come summertime when Clare meets Tipperary in the Munster championship. The rumours are that Donald will ban all Tipperary people from entering Clare. The bridge between Ballina and Killaloe will be covered with barbed wire.

I have no doubt but that the decent people of Clare will reject Donald at the polls. There might be an employment stimulus though. Donald is looking at building nuclear silos in West Clare, which is that bit nearer to the Middle East than the United States.

Ah, but if Donald only moved faster. Sure he could have bought the whole country a few years back in the middle of the recession. There would be no need for elections and Donald could have banned and bombed away to his heart's content.

In the meantime, Donald will have to make do with ruling America.

SOME OF SANTA'S TAXES HAVE BEEN VERY UNPOPULAR. ESPECIALLY THE CARBON TAX. FOR YEARS AND YEARS, THE ELVES PEED ON THEIR LITTLE FINGERS IN THE COLD WEATHER – TO KEEP WARM

37

Santa Hanging On By His Nails As Elves Make Merry

December 24, 2012

THERE will be no lap dancing in the frozen north this Christmas. The North Pole is in meltdown. Elves are downsizing. Christmas dinner this year is roast pet reindeer. Most of the toy manufacturing has been outsourced to China. A succession of tough budgets has Santa hanging on to the edge of the fiscal cliff by his fingernails.

If it wasn't for the Germans there would be no reindeer to pull the sleds. Donner and Blitzen are German, and so, too, is Rudolf. It seems if Santa defaults on his loans, the reindeer will be repossessed and he will never get a reindeer ever again. That's the way it is with banks. Santa is trapped. Have you ever tried to park a tractor and trailer on a slippy rooftop?

Eejits and demagogues proliferate. "Santa should pitch the bankers to hell," they say.

"It is not possible," replies Santa. "You must not insult the polar bear's mother before you cross the ice."

Some of Santa's taxes have been very unpopular. Especially the carbon tax. For years and years, the elves peed on their little fingers in the cold weather – to keep warm.

The leader of the elves proclaimed: "It was a classic case of taking the piss.

"I'm in favour of cuts," he said patriotically, but he would not specify exactly what or who should be cut. Santa said if the elf leader was a barber, everyone would have long hair. But no one laughed.

The elves went mad over the tax on the Reindew, or the 'old unreliable' as they call it up north. Elves can't really handle their drink and are prone to violence and cirrhosis. It's called the 'elfin gene'. "It was an attack on the family," said the spokesman for the elves. And on women who drink jars of it to pass the dark northern days.

Reindew is a potent mix of fermented walrus milk and reindeer colostrum. The shandy tastes a bit like fish finger-flavoured yoghurt.

The 'tit tax' has Santa sliding down the polls faster than a fireman on bonfire night.

The papers went mad over the cuts. Pixie columnists attacked Santa, and so, too, did North Pole TV. It's not cool in cold countries to tell the truth. Not one of the commentators mentioned the national debt. Not one even knows how much Santa has to borrow every day to run the country.

Many elves have had to emigrate to Eurodisney and take up work with Snow White as baby dwarfs. Elves are hungry and the old are always cold.

The elves, who caused all the trouble to begin with, are climbing steadily in the polls.

The people of the north have memories as short as the shortest days of mid-winter when the light lasts no longer than the on-off flick of a switch.

It was the elves who caused the property bubble. It will come as a great shock to the people of Ireland, but back in the days a two-bedroom igloo was fetching around a half a million caribou hides. Most of the new igloos were built on ice flows and the ice banks gave out credit for crazy schemes to build igloos and ice hotels in Marbella.

Their slogan was 'every elf shall have more than the next'.

The elves' biggest giveaways were the Christmas stocking bonanzas of the noughties. Elves have small feet and, therefore, wear small socks.

But that led to problems. How could you fit PlayStations 1, 2 and 3 into a Christmas stocking no bigger than a foxglove?

Simple, said the cabinet. "We'll give the elves a notional shoe size of 16" – which, in elfin terms, was as big as 5-series family sleigh. Happy days. But at what cost? It was as foolish as a cod voting for a fish-finger factory.

The elves were kicked out of government when the country went bust and the Pole people had to give up their sovereignty.

"Look at it this way," said Santa, "it's a free accountancy service." It being a well-known fact the elves are incapable of exercising any restraint when it comes to spending.

Santa cut out the Christmas stockings completely. As he said on Budget night: "If you have no socks you can't pull them up." One or two of Santa's most trusted advisers turned elf on him and gave out stockings behind Santa's back to their constituencies. The politicians' stockings are still bulging. The opposition are growing stronger by the day.

They will wait until poor Santa cleans up all the caribou poo and then when the thaw comes he will be as yesterday as Cabbage Patch Dolls and Ludo.

"Ho, ho, ho" will be heard no more. Santa will slip silently into the deathly cold, as is the way in the frozen north. And as the old man walks into the longest sleep of all, he will hear the elves' joyous singing.

Every iffy elfin making merry,
Strip every tree of every berry
Eat caribou too and reindeer stew
Guzzle gallons of Reindeer brew.
Elves and pixies spend the mostest
And let the last hour be the sorest.
Chorus
Elfin once again,
Elfin once again
And Lapland long a province be,
Will be Elfin once again.

THERE WAS THE LADY IN THE FAUX LEOPARD SKIN DRESSING GOWN WHO WAS SURE I WAS A GENTLEMAN CALLER FROM A DATING WEBSITE. "YOU'RE OLDER THAN YOUR PHOTOGRAPH," SHE SAID. "ARE YOU COMING IN ANYWAY?"

38

Sins Are Forgiven, While Service Is Forgotten

June 15, 2016

FOUR years ago here on this very spot, we forecast that the Irish people were possessed of the memory of a gnat smashed against the windscreen.

The country was ruled by the IMF and the EU. The danger was that Ireland would go in to a devastating liquidation from which we would never rightly recover.

But we were saved and nice thanks we gave. This last government freed Ireland. Fine Gael and Labour didn't help their cause though by constantly attacking Fianna Fáil and Micheál in particular over their part in our downfall. For the first time in the history of the world, politicians admitted they were sorry and made a mistake. And while many didn't forgive Fianna Fáil for selling us into slavery, many did.

Micheál Martin was calm, reasoned and personable. Martin played a blinder on the television. And all the attacks on Fianna Fáil reminded those who left Fianna Fáil for Fine Gael five years ago that deep inside they were still soldiers of destiny.

The view was formed that their former party, now reconstituted, wasn't so bad after all.

I was out canvassing for Jimmy Deenihan, which is why I didn't write here about the election as I felt there would be justifiable allegations of bias. All careers end in tears if you're a football manager or a politician. Unfortunately, Jimmy lost his seat.

The first time I met Jimmy Deenihan was at the school league final when I was in second class. Even then, he was the star.

My dad was a great friend of Jimmy's father, Mick, who was a small farmer, and Dad asked Jimmy to show me his medal. Jimmy went on to win five All-Ireland medals for Kerry and captained Kerry to win the four-in-a-row. I never missed a game. That's all forgotten now in Kerry. It's as if he never played football at all.

Jimmy went on to become a minster in the government and he worked all hours. The worst thing for a Kerry politician is to be appointed to a ministry. You get blamed for everything. We even managed to get rid of a Tánaiste and a Minster for Justice.

The excellent John Brassil took Jimmy's seat. John has the brains to become a senior minister but it's the same here in Kerry as writing out your own P45.

Jimmy was the only TD in the Dáil who was interested in the arts. He produced several films and the monies raised went to local literary causes.

The proceeds of his autobiography, €70,000 to be exact, went in to keeping the Lartigue Railway open. His Fine Gael colleague, Brendan Griffin, kept his seat. Brendan gave up half his salary to keep two teachers in their jobs in his old school.

Jimmy Deenihan played a huge role in bringing jobs to North Kerry. This has been acknowledged by several companies and I have confirmation from meetings and calls made in the preparation of this piece.

Up until this election, Jimmy had a glittering career. He is honest and he cares. In the end, the people voted him out and this is their right but I think Kerry made a huge mistake. All but 8,000 of us made a huge mistake.

In the end, Kerry put potholes before plays.

Good luck to the winners. Martin Ferris helped greatly with the peace process. I don't share his politics but he works away, all day, every day.

I met Michael Healy-Rae on the campaign. He's good fun, is Michael. Forget the bluster. Michael is very intelligent. His brother, Danny, is in at number two. A great day for the Healy-Raes.

Watch out, Michael. You are now the top man and there are politically organised pods who will target you on social media. The pods are armed not with pea shooters but with armalites full of buckshot.

The plan is that if you repeat the lie often enough, well then it will be believed. There were those who said Jimmy Deenihan did nothing. No man worked harder. It's so terribly unjust that 34 years of unceasing dedication can be dismissed by those who knew nothing of his patriotism, valour and integrity.

The Labour Party has been decimated. History will judge Labour far more sympathetically than the electorate. The Labour party signed up to cuts at a time when the country was ruled by a foreign power. Labour surely knew the people would turn on them and they did.

Our local Labour TD, Arthur John Spring, lost his seat. His uncle Eric is one my closest friends. I feel so sorry for AJ but maybe in a way the loss of the seat will lead to a new and better life for him. AJ is a good man too, from great stock. Politics is a horrible job.

My old dad was on his last legs around the time of the 2002 election but he managed to go out and vote for Jimmy. Dad was dead just a few days later. My dad warned me during those final days never to go into politics. There was no need for him to worry. I have no great desire to spend the rest of my life filling potholes.

There were lighter moments. I knocked on one door and the man inside pointed to a German flag made from manure bags. "Germany are ruling us now," he said.

There was the lady in the faux leopard skin dressing gown who was sure I was a gentleman caller from a dating website.

"You're older than your photograph," she said. "Are you coming in anyway?"

There's only so far I would go to get a vote. Even for Jimmy.

I was there with him in his kitchen on Saturday morning when the bad news came through.

He was hurt for sure but his reaction was "this is terrible

because I had more work to do for Kerry, more projects to complete."

True to form, seconds after the bad news, Jimmy made a call to a woman who asked him for help. He kept his promise, as he always has done.

I didn't have the heart to tell him the lady he was helping out just then told me she was voting Healy-Rae, one and two.

Thanks to you, Jimmy, for all you have done for us.

39

Have Mercy On Me, Angel Of Death

September 4, 2012

I WAS going to write a very sad, carefully thought-out story, about emigration and loneliness. I changed my mind just this second because of a chance encounter with the Angel of Death.

You wouldn't be the better of him. The Angel has a red nose from the booze and he feeds on human misery.

I just couldn't face into writing a sad story after listening to him.

"Did you hear about poor oul' Mikey?" the angel asks with the glee barely concealed.

I was pinned up against the wall of Spar.

"He was opened up and closed," said the Angel.

Opened up and closed is one of his favourites. He loves that one.

There's all the doctors peering into some lad's inners with a flash lamp and all of a sudden one of them shouts "quick, feck sake, will ye close him, will ye close him up quick before we catch something." And off they go sewing like mad with crochet and knitting needles.

Next he tells me a Mrs X is in the departure lounge.

"They're switchin' off the machine at noon so the doctors will be in time for their dinner," said the Angel. "She's arranging her own funeral already with the undertaker."

He loves amputations. Angel tried to load all his misery on my friend Tim O'Carroll, who lost both legs due to the same kidney condition the All Black rugby player Jonah Lomu suffers from, but Tim wouldn't let the Angel get him down.

Tim, who is still very much to the good, put an ad in the paper when he lost his first leg.

"For Sale. Six right shoes. Contact Tim O'Carroll at . . ."

It killed the Angel.

Tim is probably my all-time number one hero. Well up there with the Paralympic gold-medal winners.

If there was a gold medal for brains, being in good form nearly always and doing a fine line in humorous sarcasm, then Tim's your man.

He calls into the pub and you ask: "Well Tim, what did you get up to today?"

"Ah just arsing around, Bill."

His wife Pat looks after him so well but sometimes I think it's Tim's aversion to the American far right that keeps him alive.

Tim spent years working as a trade union man in upstate New York and he was very active in social and civil rights issues of the day. Tim always took the side of the underdog.

One day Tim barred a guy from our pub because he insulted Bill Clinton. Tim loves Clinton and Obama, too.

There's this big statue of Bill Clinton outside the garda barracks in Ballybunion. Bill is swinging a golf club and the statue was erected as a tribute to the former US president when he played on the famous Ballybunion Golf Links

This neo-fascist American called in to John B's and Tim got to arguing with him.

The American called the statue "the p***k with the stick", and Tim barred him forthwith. From my bar, and he was dead right.

I ran away from the Angel. Just ran.

Told him my bleeper was gone off.

There's a small town convention that you wait until people are finished talking to you before heading away. In a way, it's kind of nice in that everyone gets their say. It could be an old person living alone who hasn't spoken to another human being for 18 hours.

But I can't do the Angel.

Tim tried hard to get rid of him from the pub but it would be easier to saw a barnacle from a rock with a dandelion stem .

"So and so is very bad," Tim told the Angel.

The Angel's ears pointed up like a beagle on the scent of a fox and his narrow ferret's eyes came alive with the pleasure of impending death.

"What's up with him, Tim? Is it the lad, Tim? Is it, Tim? Is it the lad?"

The lad is another word for cancer.

"No," replied Tim, "it's not the lad but it's very, very serious."

"What is it then, Tim?' Is it type 2? Go on what is it? Will he be lucky to see Christmas?"

That's another great one of his. "He'll be lucky to see the Listowel Races or Easter."

Another favourite is: "They sent him home and told him they could do no more for him."

Picture all the doctors with some poor misfortune on his last legs.

"Go on," they shout. "Go on. Feck off out of it. Go on away home, will you. We can do no more for you here. Go on. Clear off will you. You're taking a bed from a lad with a chance. Next."

"Is it a stroke, Tim? Can he talk, Tim? Is his left side paralysed, Tim? Would he know me if he saw me, Tim?"

"No, it's not a stroke", replied Tim, who suffered several strokes but never complains even though he finds it difficult to read nowadays.

"What is it? Is it the bloods, Tim? Are they too thin or too thick? Have he pain when he do go to the toilet? Is his undercarriage leaking, Tim? Is he in trouble with the population stick? Go on, Tim. Tell us. Ah go on. Have he Alzheimer's? Do he know the Hail Mary in Irish? Was he ever bitten by a rat? Can he backfire? Is the liver after fallin' out with the heart?"pleads the now desperate Angel.

"Sorry," said Tim. "We cannot tell you on grounds of customer confidentiality."

But the Angel came back and he's still killing people. I swear he's going to get the road the next time he comes in to the pub. The only problem is he's related to half the country and they might stop coming in as well. Then again, I suppose mass murder is as good a ground for barring someone as anything else.

MICKEEN CAREY, UP ON A
LADDER, PAINTING A HOUSE
AT HIS EASE. MICKEEN HAD A
CAT NAMED TIBBLES WHO
COULD MEEOW *THE CLIFFS OF
DOONEEN* IN JAPANESE

| 40 |

A First Day At School

August, 2011

SHE'LL take to the bed at 10 and wonder where the years have gone.

Not her years but the five or so belonging to her little baby who went off to school today for the very first time.

Even though you know your little boy will be home in a couple of hours the pillow is wet with tears.

The teacher seemed nice enough and the boys and girls were fine even if the blonde girl who sat next to your baby kissed him on the cheek.

"They're all bitches only your mom," you feel like telling him. You know then you're being obsessive and possessive.

You realise these little kids will be his friends forever. You wonder who will be the closest ones as you scan the class.

In a few years the close ones will walk into your kitchen and help themselves to the contents of the fridge and it will not bother you in the least because they are his friends and will always be, for such it is with the kids you start out with. All reared out of the one pot and as much an influence on your child's life as anyone he is ever likely to meet in the years ahead.

It was so long ago but I have this vague recollection of my Dad taking me up Courthouse Road – my mother was too heartbroken to bring me on that first day – and there he was, Mickeen Carey, up on a ladder, painting a house at his ease.

Mickeen had a cat named Tibbles who could meeow the Cliffs of Dooneen in Japanese.

Mickeen's face was full of sympathy. It was a last look at the old order. Somehow, I sort of knew I was being launched out into a great voyage.

That's all I remember. Mrs Scanlan our teacher was nice. I know that much but other than that last look at Mickeen I cannot remember a single day in 'Babies.'

It's as if I was in a coma and missed a year of my life.

You live so much longer if you keep a diary. It's all there to be read back over when memory fades and reality turns into myth as the years pass by.

The mammy or daddy might keep one until her son grows older and then he can carry on. The entries will spark recollection and your child will live twice over.

The other tip for the first timers is to start sparing now for college.

Time flies as the man said when it took him two seconds to scroll through six months on the online airline calendar. That's how it is.

If you are grieving today, cheer up, for you too will make lifelong friends, especially if you are living far away from your native place. Up until school the mammy will feel lonely for her female companionship and then through meetings at school gates she too will develop lasting friendships. But here's a cautionary tale told to me by the principal of a big school in Belfast.

The father arrived back from his travels with a lovely bride from the Far East. She was shy but willing, both in the bedroom and in the kitchen. The tradition in her country was the woman was to do her man's bidding, no matter what. The husband was a decent sort and he loved her very much. He offered do his share of the housework.

One day he got up from the kitchen table to fetch a tablespoon and his beautiful, elfin, dusky bride was most upset he didn't ask her to get the spoon.

She collected their child every day after school while the hunter-gatherer was off out in the city earning money at his desk.

Bit by bit the eastern beauty became friends with the other

school mothers. At her husband's insistence, the perfect wife invited her new friends over for Eastern pastries so sweet and light and full of intricate, subtle flavours she never had any bother in persuading her guests to come back for afters.

The Eastern lady made many friends. After a time it could truly be said she became more Irish than the Irish themselves. Now he does his own ironing and the banker's chauvinistic friend tells him it was the bitches at the school gate who got to her.

Education is not just for kids. Mammies learn too.

You get up in the unusual stillness and blow dry his duck down pillow with a hairdryer in case the new scholar somehow cops you've been crying.

A watched clock never ticks but somehow it crawls to hometime.

Then as you wait outside the school the lollipop lady, sweating like a sumo under her big yellow coat, swears all kids are psychopaths who pay no attention to the safe-cross or any other code and you worry if you've sent him to the right school.

You tell her you've considered home schooling but you were afraid you wouldn't be able to do the maths.

The lollipop lady tells you one and one is still two as she bats a butterfly over the school wall with her big sign.

The bell rings and you rush in as quickly as Katy Taylor.

This is the first of many school reports. Maybe teacher will say your lad is a genius and they're putting him into secondary school straight away. Maybe he failed Lego.

Your heart pounds and it will pound many times over the coming years on the mornings of Leaving Certs and college exams.

He will cuddle up to you at the end of that first day when you get home. You feel reassured. He says he doesn't want to go back. It's not easy for a little boy so used to one on one, to learn how to handle one on 21.

'How long does school go on for mammy?' he asks trustingly.

You haven't the heart to tell him he has nearly 20 years to go. He's a lifer now.

Soon you will have to go back to work. Another parting. You've toiled and thought your way to get where you are now and your career is important. The money is needed to pay bills and it's only a small consolation that there are many more mammies in exactly the same situation. But you will manage, somehow, as best you can.

You read for him, the best education of all. Soon he falls asleep in your arms, exhausted from the first day. And his little sleepy head, teeming with new ideas, even in dreamtime, rests lightly on his dried out duck- down pillow.

41

A Band Of Amateurs, Poets And Romantics. We Owe Them So Much

March 28, 2016

ONE thing we do know is that there were never so many dying to die. Today, 100 years on, hundreds of thousands of the citizens of the country the revolutionaries died and helped found, pay homage to the fallen.

All around us, the debate rages.

Were those who died for Ireland in 1916 a bunch of hapless lunatics and romantics who were certain that whatever did they did God was on their side?

Or were the executed a band of brave men who loved their country and foresaw that the giving up of their lives was the only way to free Ireland? These are the questions that have come up time and again.

Yes, there was religion involved and it must have been some consolation to those who lost their lives that there was a bed in heaven awaiting them.

To compare those who were executed or killed in action to the murderous fanatics who blew up innocent people in Brussels last week is grossly unfair but there was a sense among those who took part that their quest would end in death. There's a difference between the devout and the fanatic. The 1916 fight was up-front and brave. No one can question the courage of the men who died and the women who fought alongside. They fought fair. For the most part. There are no black and whites anywhere in this story or in any other story from the backtracks of history.

The O'Rahilly – who was always a personal hero of mine –

dressed up in a specially tailored and somewhat stylish uniform. He was against the Rising not so much on any conscientious grounds but because of the timing and the lack of organisation. But he showed up.

The O'Rahilly, who was married with children, charged a British machine gun post and died on a street in Dublin. He knew the organisation of the Rising was a shambles. But he was still there to support his comrades, even though he knew he faced certain death. According to Yeats, his words were: "Because I helped to wind the clock, I come to hear it strike."

And who could not but admire the courage of James Connolly, who died strapped to his chair? Or weep at the love letters of Joseph Mary Plunkett?

Good men they were, but not perfect men. There was a terrible exploitation of children by the rebels. Schoolkids were being trained for war. They were far too young to make up their own minds. This deliberate targeting of children was a form of abuse. There's no other way of looking at it. Flawed heroes? Yes. There's a difference between child soldiers and toy soldiers. Until the days after the executions, the rebels didn't have a majority, even within the rebels. Most of the rebel forces didn't want an open battle. There was total confusion on the day. If mobile phones were around in 1916, the rising would probably not have taken place.

The truth is, 1916 was an amateur day out organised, for the most part, by poets and romantics.

Innocent civilians lost their lives and the British didn't have a monopoly on atrocity.

Red is usually given as the colour of revolution but most conflicts are grey. The rebels' cause, though, was a just one. We were an invaded country. Taken over by a foreign power who used and abused us for nearly 800 years.

There are many who say we would have won independence anyway when the war was over. I disagree. Look at Scotland. In the end, they voted to stay within the union. But that vote took place in 2015 – a long way from 1916. There would have been some compromises from the British if the rising had not taken place but we would have been a spancelled nation, unable to force our own march to self-determination.

And there were the unionists. And still there are the unionists. What were we going to do with them? The facts are that until relatively recent times, the British buttressed a sectarian state in the North of Ireland. We didn't even have 'one man, one vote'. And you're telling me they would have given us our freedom voluntarily and quickly?

Sir John Maxwell, who ordered the executions of our patriots, is often described as the accidental father of Irish freedom. The current British view , and again we speak in generalities, is that Maxwell was a maverick who had people shot without the permission of Lord Asquith, the prime minister. This recent spin and propaganda is no more than a 100-year-old cover-up.

Asquith and his government knew well what was going on. Asquith came to Ireland and stopped the executions but by then all of the signatories to the proclamation had been shot anyway.

I welcome the friendly relations between Ireland and Britain. They are a testimony to the peace process, the courage and foresight of the politicians involved and the people of both nations that we all get on so well together. It is my belief then that we would not have achieved the formation of 26 counties without the fighting in 1916.

So, did the patriots die in vain? No. Britain is no longer a colonial power and by and large is well disposed towards us as a people and a nation.

So by now we would have had our present status quo but we would have been kept waiting and waiting. Many people who are alive today would not have grown up in the free and independent state that is The Republic of Ireland but for the Rising of 1916.

The deaths of the patriots brought home to the defeated and subjugated Irish people that we were worthy of our freedom. What seems to have been forgotten is that 1916 was only 70 years after the famine. The memories of genocide were dormant until 1916. And those who fought and died made Ireland a nation once again. So today we praise the fallen who marched us on the pathway to freedom.

For me, it was the bravery of the way they died, more than their living, that entitles the lost leaders to the commemorative honours of the nation they helped found on this Easter Monday of 2016.

42

For A Long, Love-filled Life, Be Sure To Put Out The Bins And Tins

November 16, 2015

THE new girl has been in touch to ask if I can summarise the accumulated wisdom of the ages, as enunciated in these pages over a good many years. The tips are for men. But you must embrace change and understand that a woman needs to train a man to her ways

The first was a wife. That much I know for sure. The split-up was amicable because she was so delighted to get away from him – she is referred to as Herself, or d'ex. The second moved in and moved out after about a month. "Bickering" was his name for her.

There might have been a number three in England. The Man Who Knows Nothing About Women moved over for a while during the recession in search of work. I'm not certain of my facts here, but it seems he took up with a lady who owned a pet shop and kept snakes at home when they were poorly.

They're mad about animals in England and I'd only be guessing now, but I'd say he said it's the snakes or me – and she picked the snakes.

I saw him giving a woman a squeeze one time, long ago, at a dance in Ballybunion, and I'd say she'd be more comfortable with the python. He was a rough man.

The Man Who Knows Nothing About Women is very argumentative – especially if he's right. I try to help out by telling him it's not a debating society he's joined but a relationship, and sometimes you have to give in even when she's wrong. For the sake of a quiet life.

His latest partner is delighted with his progress. She reads this page every week for the essential guide to living with men written by a man for women. The new girl has been in touch to ask if I can summarise the accumulated wisdom of the ages, as enunciated in these pages over a good many years. The tips are for men. But you must embrace change and understand that a woman needs to train a man to her ways.

It matters little that your mother already trained you in. Most women will try to knock the mothering out of men. Do not resist. Just do as they say and you'll be fine.

Then when you go to see the mother she'll try to train you back to her ways. The best thing is to accept the rules of the house you happen to be in at any one time.

But do not carry stories as to the wonders of the house you have just left. Especially about gravy. Never parse another woman's gravy.

The same goes for pasta sauce and the frigging glut of frigging lasagne. You can go nowhere now without a feed of lasagne being put up in front of you. I hope "frigging" isn't a curse. That's another rule. Cut out the bad language and always praise the dinner.

I know a man who was refused sex for six months because he described homemade spaghetti Bolognese as "interesting".

Bins are the single biggest cause of discord in a relationship. Put 'em out and take 'em in. It's as simple as that. And don't wait to be asked. A sex therapist told me one time that putting out the bins is the best possible form of foreplay for women. Better even than nibbling at the lobes of their ears, she said – not that I was attending the therapist as a patient.

Here's another tip. Keep the car tidy. And another is to use the brush thing near the toilet. Empty the goldfish water.

Kill a mouse and don't go putting your pants inside your socks when you're doing it. We're meant to be ferocious hunters.

If you're inviting the boys back for a few beers, tell her first. And never, ever leave the cans around on the table after.

Mow the lawn and get hay fever after. That's another good tip.

"But never tell her you're sick," advised a man of my acquaintance.

"Die first," he said.

The man was passionate about his beliefs. "Women do believe men are useless at putting up with sickness. So the trick is to say nothing about the symptoms and let the symptoms do the talking for you. Sneeze and sniffle and maybe faint. The women are basically compassionate creatures and she will mind you and nurse you provided it is she who makes the diagnosis."

I tried to explain the context to The Man Who Knows Nothing About Women. For so long, millennia in fact, women were slaves. My great grandmothers weren't entitled to vote. So don't be telling them what to do. There are many countries in the world where woman are still slaves. There are many houses in Ireland where women are still slaves. Women have incredible stamina and a fierce work ethic. Small things can drive them nuts. Like the bins and the tins.

I have never heard a woman complain about the pain of having a baby. There are hundreds more tips, but I'd need a newspaper as thick as a telephone book to fit them all in, and maybe we'll finish up with this last one. I know there's been very little mention of money or sex, but there's time enough for that on another day.

So here's the last tip. Learn a poem and recite it when the two of you are on your own – or better again, write one for her. But there's no point in reciting love poems if you bring in half the football field on your shoes or if you leave a half-eaten banana to blacken on the window sill.

Under no circumstances leave a snail trail of butter on the marmalade – clean the knife first, and not on your jumper or on the rim of your sock.

MOSS HATED TO TALK ABOUT
THE GLORY DAYS FOR FEAR OF
BEING BRANDED BIG-HEADED.
I HAD TO DRAG IT OUT OF HIM
THAT HE WON A TRIPLE
CROWN BACK WHEN HE
WAS A GOD IN OUR EYES

| 43 |

The Happy Warrior Who Played It Hard And Fair

October 6, 2010

MOSS KEANE died at home in Portarlington with those he loved most by his side. He had a peaceful send-off. If any man deserved to go softly it was that ferocious warrior Moss Keane, for he was the gentlest and kindest of men.

I was lucky enough to spend nine months in his company when I helped with his autobiography. They were the happiest and funniest of times, just as these last few days have been the saddest.

I'd say he was dreading me writing this. When the cancer snuck up on him we did an interview, but he pulled it just before publication. Moss was right. The cancer was private but there was more to it than that. Moss didn't want to be seen to be elevating himself over anyone else. There were thousands out there in the same boat and Moss didn't feel any more important.

I pushed for him to do the piece and it wasn't in his nature to refuse anything to anyone, ever. I apologised when the black-type fever abated. Moss was lovely to me. It wasn't one of my finer moments, yet he forgave me in an instant.

If he was reading this now he'd ask: "What are you going on about all that stuff for?"

Moss hated to talk about the glory days for fear of being branded big-headed. I had to drag it out of him that he won a Triple Crown back when he was a god in our eyes.

He'd hide the ball in the bodies in front of him and lean against a side of the ruck as if it was keeping him from falling down. There was that quick peep above the top of the trenches like a fella looking out over a ditch to see if there was a car coming before he drove the cows across. Then the charge and he didn't bother to wait for the rest of the team.

He had the crowd with him, didn't he? Moss with the ball clamped under his oxter, every giant stride bringing him into a new townland, squeezing the air out of the leather as if it was as soft as the udder of an uileann pipe. Half the English team hanging off him and the other half keeping out of his way. It was a one-bull stampede.

We'd look at each other up on the terraces at the back of the goalposts and just say: "Moss," throw our heads back and get a fit of laughing in delight at his exuberance, strength and courage. He was one of us, a country boy. Wore jumpers with nobbly bits, lived in flats where the delph was never washed, kept his accent pure, drove a banger from the back seat, spoke of home often and wore green and gold when Kerry were in town. He was the man who made it okay for us GAA lads to go to rugby and feel part of it.

He had a word for all of us. "Well, oul' stock," he'd say when he couldn't remember a name. The northern boys had great time for him. Moss famously said, when the Troubles were at their worst: "There's no border in an Irish dressing room." Somehow you felt there was hope.

On the run-up to his first cap, Ulster's Stuart Mc Kinney was in the showers with Moss and noticed a piece of grass wedged between the cheeks of Moss's ass. "I see you were down home for the weekend," remarked McKinney.

Moss could always laugh at himself, but he never laughed at others. He was a very intelligent fella who could read you in a second and he could feel instinctively if you were out of sorts.

He dropped his tone and there was no hugging or any of that kind of stuff as was the way with our generation, but a genuine concern in his voice that put you at ease with yourself and the world. Somehow, you felt that if Moss Keane gave you the time of day, you couldn't be such a bad lad after all.

Moss beat the All Blacks with Munster, won a Triple Crown and shared a Five Nations. He didn't like to say too much about the games but he loved hanging out with the lads who played with him. I was his biographer but he always held something back for himself. We got on well but I think he was closest to the men he played with at Lansdowne, UCC, Ireland and Munster. And the lads he grew up with in Killarney and Currow.

Moss loved to return to Currow where there was always a welcome for him on the home farm. He loved his brothers, who are all a bit like himself – gramhair, wise and not given to panic.

Moss played for the village and then U-21 and junior for Kerry, won counties and Sigersons with UCC but he always felt he was too big for football. He told a pal in UCC that he felt like an articulated lorry trying to turn in a bathroom.

Moss came out from his shyness in college.

When UCC won a county championship he arranged for the team to visit Dr Con Murphy and Dr Brendan Lynch, interns in the Mercy Hospital who were forced to miss the celebrations due to work. Moss, an Ag student, found a doctor's coat and a stethoscope. He did the ward 'rounds'. One of the patients was from Currow. The following week he told Moss's mother that her son had a lovely bedside manner and that he was very much the better of the visit by 'Dr Keane'. The patient paid for two pints for Moss in a local pub.

There was drinking and carousing, but in 11 seasons he never missed a game for Ireland. Moss was very dedicated. He had too much respect for the jersey to go out half-ready, but he did whoop it up afterwards.

Sometimes it must have been hard to be Moss, to be funny and live up to the caricature of the boisterous Kerryman, but he always gave of himself. Fame can be a hard game, especially when you try to be nice to everyone. It took its toll. Yes he was fond of the drink, but he didn't touch a drop for years. He could stop when he had to. And he did it for his family.

You have no idea how much he loved his four girls. His daughters Sarah and Anne Marie and his granddaughter Ellie will miss him so much. I'm told they did all in their power to help him through his final months. Moss told me he'd love to see Ellie growing up. But that was not to be and that's the saddest part. It's so unfair, isn't it?

He was a great dad. Anything but strict, and his children adored him but not in a reverential way. More like friends.

His widow Anne will miss him terribly. She knew the real Moss. He had only just retired and it's very sad they didn't get more time together. Anne and himself had no secrets and they talked everything out.

I loved that man. He always tried to make you feel good about yourself and at times he hid that brilliant mind of his so as to allow those in his company to be seen at their best. He was a big man who could make himself small so as to help others appear big.

I hope I'm not making him into some sort of saint. He was a wild man in his youth, but he grew out of it. In some ways he was a saint and sinner too, but they were all venial sins. Moss was spiritual and he said his prayers. He'll go through the turnstiles without so much as his ticket being checked.

I can't imagine he's gone. We thought he was indestructible. And in a way he is. The spirit lives on. Somewhere. I'm sure of that. It cannot be that it's over now for Moss. It cannot be.

The starting stone of a cairn will be placed reverentially on Currow Hill today. Tomorrow he will be laid to rest in Portarlington, his other home.

I can see him outside the cricket club in Cardiff on a sunny day before a Heineken Cup final surrounded by his acolytes, telling yarns and everyone apparently knowing him well, even though most had never met him before. Or high up on Currow Hill with Fenton, the sheep dog, the name he took as an alias during the old GAA ban. Wellingtons on, a stick in hand marking his beat as he looked down on the valley of the meandering Brown Flesk where he fished as a small boy with his brothers.

He was larger than life and now I think, in a way, he's even larger than death. I can hear him now. "Will you cut out that oul stuff."

Don't you worry, Maurice, I'm done now. Sorry 'bout that, pal.

| 44 |

Man's Best Friends Can Be The Worst Because All Dogs Go To Heaven

November 2, 2015

I FOUND her lying face-upright outside our house. The vet said it was a massive heart attack. She was 19 in human years, which is very old in dog years. That was very good, we were told, for a Papillon.

Like I say, I didn't like her at the start. Cara was an informer. It was my custom 20 years ago to stay out late at night after I finished a long shift in our pub. I was always thrown out in good time by my mother but I did find a place where there were late drinks served. This was a gift that I have always had, ever since I first started drinking.

It was 22 years ago today when I came back to work in our pub when all else failed. So as you can imagine this is a hugely emotional day for me in that my mother and father, who gave me the chance to start over, are both gone now. You'd need something to keep you going, and I'm thinking of getting a dog.

The trick back then was to sneak in home, nice and quietly without being noticed, but Cara had woken up the whole house. I tried to bribe her with bits of meat and even sweets. She nearly took my fingers off to get at the meat and the sweets. Cara ate them on the spot and by way of gratitude she kept on barking.

It wasn't that I stayed out late every night, just now and then, but Cara put an end to the surreptitious drinking.

She was for my good and we became great friends. The little Papillon with her floppy ears would wait up until I came home, and sometimes I would bring her for drives in the car to the beach even though she was afraid of the waves. She had human eyes and when Cara looked up at you there was an understanding there somewhere inside of her in a place that, for all our science and biology, we have yet to discover.

Cara was gutsy and kept bigger dogs out of the garden. She even scared off the red fox living up at the top of the wood. That fox was as tall as a greyhound pup and he was the early morning lord of the garden until Cara bluffed him out of it. I had to rescue her from fighting with two huge killer grey crows. Low types they are too, with no sweet song and an insatiable desire for meat.

The kids would pull and drag at Cara and catch her by the tail but never once did she lose her temper or snap. Cara was patient and caring.

The little dog with the floppy ears and the brown and white dappled coat picked up on the mood of the house and if there were problems she tried to cheer us up by jumping up on the seat next to us.

The kids were heartbroken when she died. We buried Cara under a tree in the garden. Here's one for you, if you have lost a beloved pet and it helps the kids to get over the death. We put up a plastic headstone attached to a last post. I wrote the epitaph myself. The requiem reads: "Cara you were well named." Cara is the Irish for friend.

We didn't get another dog since.

Then today, as I was walking down the town, I met a man who is nearly always in good form but this morning he was very down. "Our little dog was killed by a car. The kids are heartbroken."

We talked for a while there on the side of the street under the statue of St Patrick and the man said he was never again going to get another dog. I knew how he felt.

But by the end of the conversation he had talked himself round to getting a new dog. "For the kids' sake."

And so it was I put it to the family that we should replace Cara. There's a debate going on. I was always mad about Border Collies.

I love their athleticism and their temperament above all. I'm not gone on big savage dogs descended from wolves.

Butch Browne was the first collie I knew well. We were great friends. I was his owner's butcher boy and Butch went everywhere with me. Eric Browne, who was Butch's owner, is a natural with dogs. He got it from his dad, Berkie. It seems Berkie had a special whistle and when he tooted half the dogs in town came along with him for a walk. Dogs love Eric. One look from him and they know what they should do.

Once when another pal of mine was asked to take his dog out of a restaurant, he was highly indignant which as you all probably know, is even more indignant than indignant. Said my friend to the management team: "She is better bred than half of ye, and she has better manners than the other half of ye."

Patsy Hickey, who drove the trains in England, lost his little dog this day last week and he says he's not sure if he'll get another dog due to being "so lonesome after them when they're gone." Another friend was grieving for her late dad's old dog.

I asked Eric to be on the look-out. Just to see. No decision has been made yet. He's says he'll try for a collie as well bred as Butch, whose grandmother starred on 'One Man and His Dog'.

MOST IRISH LADS THINK THE CLITORIS IS A PERENNIAL BLOOM THAT THRIVES IN THE SHADE AND SANDY SOIL

45

A Guide To The Intricacies Of The Female Form From A Thoroughly 'Modern Man'

September 7, 2015

I SUPPOSE we only have ourselves to blame. Men, that is. For years, the Irish definition of foreplay was "pull across the curtains".

Then you phone the lads down in the pub to tell them you won't be long. And make sure you say to tell the barman to start a nice creamy pint of Guinness. "Sure won't it be settled by the time I'll be done here with herself."

The mighty lover gives his all for the full three minutes, about the time it takes a pint to get pulled, rested, topped up and settled.

I often wonder is that the reason why Irishmen only take the bare three minutes to make love.

Although I'm not too sure if there's much love involved in a physical enterprise lasting no longer than the time it takes for a pint to travel from tap to lip.

Are we somehow subconsciously programmed to give three minutes to most matters involving partners, such as serious talks and the like?

Serious talks as in when the woman asks the man to come down to the room in the house no one goes. Men dread serious talks in the room no one uses. The worry room, they call it.

Maybe if the men gave more time listening to their partners' concerns, well then we wouldn't be about to be made redundant.

So here's what's going to happen in the future – but the future is now. The pill is almost ready to go on the market. I'll bet there was no shortage on volunteers for the clinical trials.

The new woman will buy a nice bottle of red, a packet of Mariettas and sit herself down by the fire, all on her own.

Then she'll pop an orgasm pill as she gets a fierce fit of laughing at the pathetic efforts of her previous boyfriend to find the G-spot. She only dated him because he was a mechanic and thought, wrongly, that because of his expertise in servicing the internal combustion engine, he would have no bother at all in figuring how to best figure the inner workings of a woman.

I know that by now the 77.3 million men, or thereabouts, worldwide, who read this column with a view to learning more about themselves and their mates will have labelled me a traitorous wretch who panders to women.

But I say better a panderer than a philanderer and here's one, or even two for ye now, boys.

Do ye take golf lessons? And by any chance did any of ye ever go down to the local community college of a winter's evening to do a night class on motor maintenance? And would you keep the dog up on your lap for ages rubbing him and stroking him and rubbing again and talking to him in baby voice and saying stuff like 'Who's a good fella?' and 'Aren't you my best friend?' and would you buy him treats like tasty bits of meat and the like?

Well would you?

Go on now.

Tell the truth, and would you give hours to studying the horses round Cheltenham time?

I even heard tell of a man who learned how to knit off old Woman's Ways.

Okay, so we've established that men take the time to be affectionate to dogs and to learn all about how complex machines work and to study car manuals and the like and to read the assembly instructions in Mandarin for making up of hard-to-fix-up stuff like trampoline-type things for the kids.

Well how many of you have taken up orgasm-giving lessons? None, I'd say.

It's like the horrible, horrible old misogynist joke: "How do you give a woman an orgasm?" And the answer: "Who cares?"

And don't go saying ye would if they were available in the community college. Because if enough men kicked up enough of a fuss, the courses would go ahead.

It might not be too late for this year's season of night classes. Maybe you could cancel the 'Mechanics Made Easy' and 'How to Fix Mobile Phones with Dental Floss' courses.

So that's why the female orgasm pill was invented – because men had no interest whatsoever in the female orgasm or how it's made or even where it lives or if it exists at all.

Don't say I didn't warn ye. Fully two years ago in this very column, we did tell ye. We did.

Here's just one line of the column that was completely ignored.

"Most Irish lads think the clitoris is a perennial bloom that thrives in the shade and sandy soil."

I'll bet ye're sorry now. It used to be men were needed for physical labour.

The women nowadays are getting strong again, physically that is. They were always strong mentally.

What with going to the gym and lifting kettle bells, the women don't need us to put out the bins any more.

As is always the case when a new invention comes in, there was no thought given to economic fall-out.

When the internet was invented, did we ever think that it would close down Main Street? So what about the men and women working in the vibrator factories? Their jobs are surely at risk, although there may well be a positive spin in that the wifi might improve. But then that will put the TV and wifi repairers out of business.

Is it too late to have the orgasm tablet banned?

Will men be given one last chance?

I DREAM NOW OF A UNITED
IRELAND AND OF TRAVELLING
BACK UP NORTH WITH
MICKEY WHEN OUR RIVERS
REALLY DO RUN FREE

46

Fifty Years On, 'Only Our Rivers Run Free' Is Still Flowing Beautifully Along

August 10, 2015

MICKEY MacCONNELL was barely 18 when he wrote 'Only Our Rivers Run Free'. That was 50 years ago this week.

Mickey's anthem has been translated into 30 languages and there are hundreds of recordings. Most of us know the chorus and the song is sung at least once at every pub sing-a-long. The young boy's ballad about the Troubles in his home place has the test of time.

Mickey maintains that there is hardly a man or woman from the North who hasn't been damaged by the terrors of a long war.

"It is my honest belief that all of my generation who grew up in the North during the Troubles were maimed, dwarfed and diminished in myriad ways. We are all survivors of death and madness and are all individually damaged in many ways."

He found redemption and some peace in his music and his family. There was so much fun too that you'd be bursting to meet up.

We travelled to Donegal for a festival in Culdaff, a small village with a big heart. We drank and talked. Two days it took, and if you add in the two days travelling up, well then that made four, plus three in Culdaff.

I knew the real Mickey after that trip. I told him about my troubles and he told me about the Troubles. For me, he is a mix of an older brother and a father-confessor.

By way of a peace offering, I gave a present to Mickey's wife Maura. It was a holy picture of Padre Pio, bought in Knock, where we stopped for a cure. Padre Pio was drained and worn from losing all that blood. Maura said Mickey looked even worse.

Maura keeps Mickey going and tries to mind him by throwing parties at every conceivable opportunity. They have two daughters, Clare and Kerry, named by Maura after the counties where the girls were conceived. Mickey loves his three girls. And they love him.

They're great sport and my heart lifts when the family come into the pub. And his brothers are so brilliantly musical, so generous and so gentlemanly.

The healing is ongoing, though. There are confidences that will never be broken. Suffice to say Mickey was of his time and of his people.

As he says himself: "There was no middle ground back then. You were either with us or against us." And yes, the North cracked him, but he never broke.

'Only Our Rivers Run Free' was written out of a seething anger at the way our people up North were being treated by a regime that denied a minority the most basic of civil rights, such as one man, one vote.

I'm never really at ease when it comes to writing about the Troubles. You can never really understand why people were forced to take up arms to defend their families until you've been through it.

I worked for three days a week in the North about 20 years ago. It was then I saw our people looked South for back-up, but it never came. We blew bugles for sure, but there was no cavalry.

I'm not talking about violence here. I was never for that. My heroes were John Hume and Séamus Mallon. For most of us, the North really was a foreign country, best ignored and a problem never to be solved.

Maybe we never knew how much you loved us. The young boy's song was a cry for help.

Oh where are you now when we need you?

What burns where the flame used to be?

Are you gone like the snows of last winter?

The older Mickey still remains "unapologetically republican" but he's all for the peace now. "I don't want my kids and grandkids to go through what we went through." He is ashamed at times of the crimes committed in the name of republicanism.

Mickey settled in Listowel with Maura back in the 1970s. "I came for a fleadh cheoil and never went back."

When we first met, years ago, I was the conservative know-all, "surely destined for high office", who was certain all republicans were bloodthirsty killers.

Mickey had an image of me as someone singing 'Faith of our Fathers' on the dockside for General O'Duffy as he sailed away to make mayhem in Spain.

I dream now of a united Ireland and of travelling back up North with Mickey when our rivers really do run free.

But he is annoyingly self-deprecating. When Mickey sings 'Only Our Rivers' in John B's, he introduces the song by announcing: "And now for a medley of my greatest hit." We will do another piece on another day about the 50 and more masterpieces he has written.

Mickey wrote the song for his father when he saw defeat in his Dad's eyes for the first time. It was at a riot in Enniskillen, when the bad men of the B Specials were beating up nationalists randomly and without provocation.

Mickey was driven by a fierce sense of social justice. He became a courageous journalist and columnist, who wrote so beautifully for so many years. He saw his song-writing as part of his campaign his campaign to right wrongs.

Christy Moore recorded a superb version of Mickey's masterpiece. Soon enough 'Only Our Rivers Run Free' became the theme tune of the civil rights movement.

Fifty years ago, a young lad's song for his father became the anthem of a dispossessed people.

We'll finish now with a verse from Mickey.

When apples still grow in November,
When blossoms still grow from each tree
When leaves are still green in December
It's then that our land will be free.
I wander her hills and her valleys,
And still through my sorrows I see,
A land that has never known freedom
And only her rivers run free.

47

Ireland Is A Home At Last For Us All, A Home With A Heart

May 25, 2015

HOME now with you now, and no looking over the shoulder. That day is gone, gone and forever. Pick up your step, and walk in time to the beat of a nation's heart. For home is where the heart is. Lift up the latch and in with you. You are home now.

Home at last.

There was a difference in him. A new confidence, as he strolled down Church Street. It was the jaunty walk of the young boy on his way home from school on the first day of the summer holidays. The walk of the captain going up to collect The Sam Maguire. The walk of lovers marching up the aisle. Here come the grooms. Here come the brides.

"Hey Bill," he said, "there's no more gay or straight any more. We are all the one."

Home at last.

It was at the count centre in Tralee and I met Rena Blake and Lisa Fingleton. They have the lovely Listowel Arms booked for their Civil Partnership in July. We hope the wedding laws will be changed in time. Their smiles told it all. "We won, we won. And by so much."

Jim Kenny has all the tallies.

"How was Listowel?" I ask.

My heart is pounding. Lisa and Rena go silent now.

One box was 74pc yes. My home town, in the heart of rural Ireland, was a landslide yes.

I fell in love with Listowel all over again.

And I thought of one of my nearest and dearest who had to hide his sexuality back in the days when gay love-making was punishable by imprisonment.

He can come home to a proper home now, and not just a shelter from the wind and cold. Your name is on the town deeds, my old pal. Home, home at last.

There were many too who voted No. It wasn't as if there was a homophobia epidemic.

Most of the older Nos just didn't know any gay people. But they did. They did. It was just that the gay people were too petrified to let their sexuality be known. Several generations passed by and there was never the chance for heart to hearts, like we have today.

If there was an open day at Aine and Honor Hurley's house then they wouldn't have been so scared of change. The girls can marry now. Their kids are lovely. The home is as happy as any I've ever been in. When last I checked, they looked just like me and you.

In time there will be football matches and concerts and birthday parties and mammy chats at the school gate.

The doubters will become converts. It is time now for new conversations. A time for learning, on both sides. A time for the Nos to ease gradually into the new Ireland like a favourite fireside chair.

A time for gay Ireland to keep on canvassing, long after the votes have been counted. In the end, the vote wasn't so much about marriage or surrogacy or adoptions or constitutions, but acceptance.

So many who came out were still suffering from varying degrees of post-traumatic stress brought on by the years of living in fear and loneliness.

They were pretty sure Ireland had changed but reassurance was needed. Even on polling day when stories of the high poll were coming in, gay people were saying: "If we win by just one vote..."

They weren't sure. The minority, as ever, were depending on the majority for equal rights. Our gay Irish craved reassurance.

I was told of the story of the mother who went to Medjugorje to have her gay son cured of his gayness when Knock failed her, and of the brothers who tried to beat the gayness out of their sibling.

Our gay Irish are cured forever now, and they are still gay.

The three gay friends who joined me for a drink on Saturday night were exhausted from the emotion of it all. If their tears of joy were metered, the boys would never be done paying off Irish water.

I noticed the gay men were unconsciously taking in deep, long breaths until there were bubbles on the tips of their toes. It was as if my three friends were breathing in the fresh air of freedom.

I just never knew. Me, who was so sure I knew just what my gay friends were going through. I suppose when you've been a second-class citizen for so long, it takes a while to get used to freedom. The half-way house is vacant now.

I am so proud to be Irish. So proud of the young Irish. So proud of our kids who travelled home to vote. There's so much hope for Ireland. If our young people care, then we will prosper, and our island can become a nation of illumination once again.

The mothers won it for us. Mary McAleese led the way. The Irish mothers had the compassion and the foresight. A No campaigner told us at the count of the mothers who refused their petition for a No with a "what if I have a gay child or a gay grandchild, well then is it fair they should be made to feel different?"

My mother is 86 and we watched the good news surge out of the television. I will never forget the moment the result was called out. It was as if Ireland was freed all over again, in the very place where Michael Collins took Ireland back from the British.

So there we were, Mam and me, with our biscuits and our tea, and our happy tears for the free.

THE LONE COUNTRY SHOP ON
THE SIDE OF THE ROAD IS ALL
BUT GONE AND THAT IS SO
SAD. THESE OUTPOSTS OF
COMMERCE WERE MUCH MORE
THAN JUST THAT. THEY WERE
A DROP-IN CENTRE FOR
ANYONE AND EVERYONE

48

Man The Barricades
In Fight For Rural Ireland

February 11, 2010

PICTURE the scene: the church gate; a collection; the usual two or three altruists. The words scrawled in red marker on a piece of cardboard stuck to the rickety table read: 'For the starving publicans.'

Let me first of all say we are not starving. We can always make a porter cake from the slops. But things are bad and the reason is not just the random breath testing.

Let's face it, we cannot complain too much about random breath testing by the guards if lives are being saved on the roads. Alright, a little bit of common sense might go a long way. We all know the danger time is late at night and we cannot expect much sympathy if we take a chance on driving with too much drink.

You would have to feel for older people living alone. It's very hard for them to adjust to the new regime. An old friend who is now gone to a place where drinks are always on the house had a few too many one night. I insisted on driving him home in his own car as he would be housebound without it. We arrived safely at his home where he invited me in for a drink. I was unable to refuse. When it was time for me to go my friend said: "Hold on a minute until I get my coat and I'll drive you home."

And it's not just the old folk who suffer. Many young parents are so weighed down by mortgages they cannot afford a night out.

Yes, 'the times they are a changin',' and fast.

The plight of the rural publicans and the communities they serve has been on everyone's lips in recent weeks. Even city folk who regard rural Ireland as one vast national park, inhabited by too-cute yokels who are subsidised to the hilt, are taking notice. And this is a good thing coming out of a bad thing.

The many commentators and politicians who have spoken on the topic seem to have missed one crucial point and it is this: Every small business in the country is under pressure. There are just too many hidden charges

Take the pubs. We have to pay four different organisations for the television alone. There's the licence, then you have Sky, Setanta and IMRO, the copyright people, have to be paid as well. We fork out for four bins: one for brown glass, another for green, a third for white bottles and a fourth for rubbish. You can imagine the space they take up.

The council even upped the cost of going to the toilet by 20 per cent when water charges went up and if we want to put a sign outside up on our wall it's €600 a year plus insurance.

And its not just the pubs who are suffering.

Small farmers are as good as gone. A farmer who was regarded as a big farmer 10 years ago is now just barely hanging in there. Where once you had fields and families you now have acres of forestry. And no criticism for selling – the farms had become uneconomic.

The lone country shop on the side of the road is all but gone and that is so sad. These outposts of commerce were much more than just that. They were a drop-in centre for anyone and everyone.

My mother came out of one such emporium. There was no greater joy than to visit Uncle Jim and Auntie Lena. There was never any shortage of sweets and the same hospitality is there today even though Jim and Lena retired a few years back.

That shop was opened by my great grandfather and, if I might just say, no person was ever left stuck in bad times. I am so proud to have the back breeding of the O'Connors behind me.

Rural Ireland is under threat as never before from the great monster in the East. Dublin is eating up all our resources. The cost of a few hundred metres of motorway in Dublin would get a small village back on its feet in Kerry. The cost of a tunnel would get every small town and village in the county buzzing.

But all is not lost.

The government has introduced some marvellous schemes and organisations such as North Kerry Together are channelling vital resources into rural Ireland.

Our leaders have let us down though. They have been reactive rather than proactive. The initiative on providing night time rural transport is a case in point.

At least Eamonn Ó Cuiv tried, and men like John O'Donoghue really do care, but what we need is a long-term strategy and this planning must be taken out of the hands of the politicians.

The government seem incapable of planning beyond whatever daily emergency presents itself. Decentralisation was an excellent idea, but it was not thought through. We must establish a forum with teeth. Get a high profile chairman who will scare the politicians, someone like Gay Byrne. Let's tell it as it is and then offer real solutions. The owners of houses in Dublin should be targeted. They should be encouraged to sell their homes in the city and move to the country. It would be a win-win situation. The seller would pocket a huge amount, get rid of the millstone mortgage and have more than enough left over to build a new home and start up a new business.

Technology has shortened the journey from Kerry to Dublin to two seconds. Enterprise offices could be set up all over the city with well-trained people who could advise and facilitate people who would like to move.

Yes, there is hope.

We have one priceless asset that can never be marginalised or taxed and that is the indomitable will of the people. There are black spots, I know, but we have a good education system. Most of our young people love their native place and after the usual few years of wandering nearly all would like to return and treat their families to the freedom of living in rural Ireland.

We in Kerry have survived calamities such as the famine, 800 years of British rule and emigration. And we will be there in 100 years time, but only if we fight the good fight. Join something that will help your community. Go on, do it now. It's time to man the barricades.

49

Men Must Probe The Benefits Of Putting Health Before Modesty

Kerryman, March 1, 2009

ALL three men were of course doctors and I was a guest at a medical dinner in Cork just last weekend.

One surgeon fixed up a hernia I picked up from rescuing a drunk who was flung down outside a chipper. The Good Samaritan in me has a lot to answer for. The second op was for the removal of an appendix and string of intestine long enough to send to Clonakilty for filling with black pudding.

And it dawned on me how lucky I was to have been looked after by three such fine gents and how lucky I was to have been talked into going to the doctor in the first place. I was sent for my first colonoscopy a few years back. The procedure involves the insertion of a camera into an orifice where the sun don't shine.

Fortunately, there's a sedative and you are asleep for the procedure. I was my doctor's football trainer and, just as he was about to take the snap, he said: "I will get my own back now for all those push ups you made me do." But it was fine. Honestly. No pain involved.

I woke up in a recovery room. I recognised a voice behind the screens just next to me. It was a friend from Cahersiveen. We were still on a bit of a high from the sedative.

I am told we sang a verse of The Boys of Barr na Sraide and even had enough presence of mind to speak the words "hunting for the wren" at the end as is the time honoured fashion in the lovely town that hugs the mountain.

The man behind the screen on the right wasn't in such good

form. He was from west Cork. An oldtimer. The kind who has his dinner at half 11 and drinks his tea out of a saucer. And he reminded me very much of a man from just outside Listowel who was asked by a nurse in the old St Catherine's if he had pyjamas. "No," was his reply. "It's a hernia I'm here for."

My pal from the south was always a bit of a joker; he told the old timer he could have the rear-end photo mounted and framed. The west Cork veteran ignored him and came out with a classic — he wasn't half as naive as we thought he was. "Boys," he groaned. "I don't envy dem gay lads wan bit of their fun."

Every one was relaxed. Our doctor, Billy Stack, is one of our own and never let his elevation in life alter his fundamental modesty and niceness. We were given tea and a biscuit and a half an hour later the three of us were discharged.

There was no pain and, in my case, it did lead to surgery but there were no further complications. But, on the whole, I felt much better afterwards.

I think it's fair to say that while the public might give out about a two-tier health system and Mary Harney battles with the profession, most of us have the height of respect for our own doctors. For that reason, there's no real excuse for the unwillingness on the part of many men to go to the doctor.

I know of one case where a young lad had pain in his testicles but was too embarrassed to go to the surgery. He died from testicular cancer and this was an intelligent well-educated young lad who could have been saved if he looked after himself in time.

Why are men so reluctant to go for prostate exams and the like while women see invasive procedures such as smear tests as merely routine? Don't know? Just go.

We owe it not just to ourselves but to our loved ones. A man will service his car every 10,000 miles but will not get himself into his GP for an overhaul. I cannot figure it out. It's a well-known fact that early detection saves lives.

I have often heard women say that men make bad patients and

we have a low pain threshold. "If men could have babies there would be no children" is an oft-quoted example.

Girls cut it out.

If your man has a pain, listen to him and do not be dismissive. Send him to the doctor. Do whatever it takes. Refuse to peel his spuds, withdraw conjugal rights or switch off the telly when Munster are playing.

We tend to categorise men who complain about their health as moaning hypochondriacs We are stigmatised as being in some way being unmanly if we look after ourselves. If you give a peep in at medical waiting areas there are always more women than men in the room.

There was a bit in my dad's hilarious book, 'Letters of a Matchmaker,' concerning a groom who had trouble with 'the population stick' in the days before Viagra. His frustrated wife advised him to go to the doctor.

He refused .

"I'll let no man look at my apparatus until I am being washed for the grave." Behind all the humour there was always a message in my dad's work. Make the appointment. And make him make that appointment.

IMPURE THOUGHTS WERE A SIN BACK THEN. MOST PEOPLE NOWADAYS WOULD CONSIDER SUCH DAYDREAMING A DELIGHT BUT, IN THE OLD DAYS, PEOPLE DID GUILT

50

Coming Clean No Longer A Penance

Kerryman, October 29, 2009

'**B**LESS me Father for I have sinned. It is 25 years since my last confession." It is true. Twenty-five years as they sing in that cringe dirge, The Boston Burger, "is a mighty long time".

But what would the priest say to me if I made a comeback? I have a funny feeling I would be well-treated. Churches are like banks; it's the customer they do not have whom they most covet. Ah but where do I start with the old sins? I would keep the poor priest in the box for a month if I went through every sin.

Jimmy Boylan was a Corkman who came to Listowel every year on his holidays. He hadn't a whole pile of time for the Church. And could you blame him? Jimmy was walloped by an assortment of priests and nuns when he was taken into care after his mother had a stroke. But he still believed in God and the sacraments. "It's the langers who dishes 'em out I have the problem with."

Over a period of time, Jimmy became very friendly with that mighty man, our curate Fr Michael O'Doherty, and he presented himself for confession.

It was nearly 50 years since Jimmy previously confessed and, even then, he held back in case the priest would wallop him savagely afterwards.

Michael O'Doherty was well before his time. He mixed freely and enjoyed a pint in the local pubs. Jimmy was put at ease and came out of the confessional as cleansed as if he was dipped in Jeyes Fluid bought in a hardware store in Knock and scrubbed with a divine wire brush purchased in a huckster's shop in the Garden of Gethsemane.

I was only a small lad at the time (I still am) but I knew poor

Jimmy was terrified of having to tell the long list of sins he had accumulated over the years.

Around this time, some psychologist discovered in the course of his research that men think of sex every eight seconds. In Kerry it is 16 seconds. Football is the reason.

Impure thoughts were a sin back then. Most people nowadays would consider such daydreaming a delight but, in the old days, people did guilt. Jimmy was in his sixties by then. How could he tell even as grounded a man as Fr O'Doherty he had seventeen billion, six hundred and seventy three thousand impure thoughts?

But Jimmy was a Corkman and, naturally, he found a way around the problem...

"What did you tell him?" asked my father out of devilment as much as curiosity. After 50 years Jimmy's confession was four words.

"I done it all."

But, alas, not all the clergy are as enlightened. I had the misfortune to endure a sermon from a priest who sees life through a veil of tears. And it was only a couple of years ago. I swear this is true.

Guess what he told the congregation?

"If ye go to the churchyard 11 times in the month of November ye will free a soul from limbo."

Limbo, for those of you fortunate enough to have escaped religious education in the old days, is a sort of halfway house between heaven and hell. It's for sinners who didn't do the bad stuff like murder, ménages à trois and the like.

And we have priests who deny the sacraments to parents who have not married. When will they ever learn? Do they not realise it's the child they are really hurting? I think, though, it is fair to say the vast majority of the current flock of clergy are decent men and women who are not afraid to show they too are human.

Most of the bad ones have been rooted out and almost all the child molesters have been decommissioned or put behind bars.

That said, we are badly in need of a reformation.

Your local priest may well be 50 to 100 years ahead of official Church policy.

The Catholic lawmakers are as out of step as a man whose lace gets caught in the moving parts of an escalator. Did you know contraception is still a sin? No one takes much notice in the developed world but the poor people in Africa do and millions die of aids while condoms stay in the wrappers. It is not all that long ago that contraception was illegal in Ireland while mothers who were warned by their doctors not to have any more kids died in childbirth. It is a shocking indictment of the Pope and his cohorts. Then and now.

The priests we deal with on a daily basis have evolved far more than the old fogies in the upper echelons over in Rome. And it is our local priests and nuns who have to carry the can for the ruling classes.

Some time soon I might write on the barbaric practice of enforced celibacy but today my dearly beloved brethren we are gathered here to discuss confession.

My favourite confession was a first.

As most of you are aware the concept of sin as outlined to the young has changed dramatically in recent years. Now instead of confessing mortal and venial sins the kids detail how they 'hurt God.'

It's a lovely ceremony with some great songs and a good bit of banter by the priest.

The kids go up to the padre, who sits smiling on the altar, and not closeted away in some dark confession box. The children are allotted a maximum of four sins – sorry, ways they may have hurt God.

A young lad from near here was the scourge of the neighbourhood. He was a good lad but he was the crossest boy ever born. However, he too had to face his day of judgement.

"Well," I asked of the small boy, "how did you get on at the first confession? And what were your four things you told the priest?"

"Cursin... fightin'... kickin'... and spittin'."

| 51 |

Life-long Talker Had It All Said In The End

November 12, 2013

GOT the bad news in Germany. In a picturesque little town on the banks of the Moselle the Americans forgot to bomb. My first cousin, Michelle, called me. I can't say it was a shock. Uncle Michael had a bad stroke a week earlier and we were told he would never recover. He was unable to communicate and was unconscious.

Michael was 84. I suppose it was a good enough age. I was reminded of the words my dying grandfather, Bill, said to my dad. "I had a great gallop, John." And Michael too got the run of the race.

I was very fond of Mike and it was a great honour when Michelle asked me to do the funeral oration. I had two worries. One was I would be struck by a bolt of lightening as I alighted the high altar of Donnycarney Church and the other was that I might not get home in time.

I travelled by boat, taxi, bus, driverless train and plane. I had plenty of time to figure out what I was going to say. On the bus from Hahn to Frankfurt I was sat beside a Venezuelan engineer.

We got chatting and I told him the purpose of my journey. He said: "Your uncle, where will he go? 'Heaven or hell?'"

Unhesitatingly, I gave Uncle Mike the thumbs up. This would be the main theme for my sermon.

Fr Corry set the tone. The church does death very well. He spoke of how Uncle Michael used to fall asleep on his visits and when my aunty Joan apologised the good father said: "If a man isn't entitled to fall asleep in his own house, well it's a poor state of affairs."

Before I spoke, Mike's grandson, Cillian, said Michael "wasn't a good granddad, he was a great granddad". Cillian told of how he and his little sister, Aisling, "loved granddad's stories about the man who lived under the bed. And he always stood to them before they left. There wasn't a dry eye in the house. I was next up. There were no notes and here's the best recollection of what I said:

"Michael wouldn't have wanted too much sadness here today. He had a good life and was a very happy man. He was, of course, a fanatical Kerry football supporter and I would liken this Mass to his going up the steps to collect the Sam Maguire on All Ireland final day. He loved his home and his family but Michael lived a secret life too. He often slipped off for a surreptitious drink or a bet and in the course of his meanderings he would meet hundreds of people. And could he talk? It took an hour to walk a hundred yards with him in his beloved Listowel.

Uncle Michael worked in the Department of Education after he left the army where he single-handedly kept Hitler at bay during The Emergency.

There were tales of derring do with secretaries, under secretaries, permanent secretaries, over secretaries and even ministers in the Department.

But Uncle Michael always came out on top.

Indeed it could be said of him he had no enemies. He was that good-natured he would forgive any slight and was absolutely non-judgemental.

Uncle Michael loved his job and felt he was contributing to the betterment of modern Ireland. He was a true patriot.

Mike loved his family above all else. Michelle, his daughter, was always daddy's little girl. He was very proud of her successful career as a teacher and now as principal. Michelle was the practical one over the days of her Dad's dying but it was a practicality based on love and respect.

She has been magnificent.

Uncle Michael would never have lasted as long but for his wife, Joan.

He was fed like a champion greyhound. I'd say there were often days when he had three or four dinners.

And if at times she handed out yellow cards when my uncle exceeded his quota she never had any intention, ever, of going for the red. My beloved uncle knew exactly how much he could get away with and Joan knew exactly how far she would let him go. Mike loved Joan so very much and it was always reciprocated."

Brendan is a great son. He and Michael were particularly close. The respect they showed each other was based on a deep understanding of each other's needs.

It was fitting that Brendan found his dad on the day of the stroke. Any of us who are the fathers of sons would take the relationship between the honest man in the coffin here beside me and his fine son down below in the front pew as the perfect father son combination.

When I called to see Uncle Michael only a few days ago I was trying to think of something that would console Brendan and Michelle and her lovely husband, Peter, who were standing sentinel beside his bed.

They were so sad because Uncle Michael couldn't speak and, for him, talk was everything.

And then it dawned on me.

I knew why he was taken. There was no need for Mike to speak any more. That gentle caring man with a smile as wide as the estuary of the Feale never stopped talking for 84 years. And that was the reason he was off to join the rest of the gang.

His epitaph is simple enough, but true: "He had it all said."

There were things I didn't say on the altar like how Mike wrote to me with words of encouragement when I started to write and lacked confidence. I will miss the handwritten letters most with the several PSs and the add ons taking up every inch of the pages. He was funny was Uncle Michael.

After the mass a tall man approached me. Bill from west Cork was a good friend and neighbour of Mike's. One hot summer, Mike was cutting the hedge at the front of the house. It was a job he hated "If you keep cutting that hedge it will die," Bill advised. "That's the general idea, Bill," was Mike's reply.

I'd say Mike sent him over to me. The hearse got a small bit lost in the cemetery, which was that big it was indeed a necropolis, the city of the dead. And Uncle Mike was at it again. I'm sure he put the words in my mouth because I certainly wasn't thinking funny thoughts. "Michelle," I mediumed as the funeral directors searched frantically, "I think they've lost the plot." Maybe he put in my mouth to cheer her up. It worked a little bit anyway. Still at it Mike, talking. Right to the very end.

52

'Just A Garda' Doesn't Have A Bubble To Retreat To When Going Gets Tough

October 19, 2015

IT was a Friday night and there was danger in the air. The men were drunk or drugged and the women were driving them on. Why this was happening I really do not know.

The drunk and doped men began to fight. It was vicious. There were no rules here. Kicks and headbutts had blood spurting and as one lad fell to the ground from a vicious punch. I could see the eyes rolling around in his head. I thought he was dead. You could hear the dull thud as his skull cracked off the pavement. More blood.

I called the gardaí. There were a couple more people on the phone too. My guess is they were also dialling 999.

For our own safety, we had to step back. Our consciences were clear in our minds. We delegated to the police. It was their problem now.

She was maybe 25 at most. Even with her peaked cap, you could see she was a pretty girl and always at times like this, dads think of their own daughters.

I could see her draw a big breath and in she went to the middle of the brawl. They were big men, the fighters. Very big. The drugs gave them the kind of crazy strength. She was just a girl. Not just a girl, just a garda.

That deep breath was a 'here goes' breath. In she went with her two male colleagues. She was shouting: "Stop!" and "There's no one dead!" and somehow her voice and the presence of her colleagues seemed to bring some order. One of the animals involved in the fight didn't stop. He made for the young girl. 'Just A Girl' caught him with her baton on his thigh.

Down he went screaming and roaring about police brutality. Maybe he wasn't going to hit her but what was 'Just a Girl' to do? She had no choice in the circumstances.

Two of the fighters were handcuffed and put in the back of the police van. It took six gardaí to subdue one of them. There was a garda each holding a kicking leg and two gardaí held on to his flailing hands. Another kept his pals at bay.

'Just A Girl' opened the door of the police van. The crazed man managed to kick her in the abdomen, but she stuck to her task and soon enough he was decommissioned.

'Just A Girl' was hurt, though. And I thought: "I hope she's not expecting." She could have been pregnant, I feared.

The years passed by and 'Just A Girl' became 'Just A Woman'. She has kids now. And then one day I heard she was badly beaten up in the line of duty. 'Just A Woman' was out of work for several months. But now she's back on the beat.

She wouldn't let the bad lads get the better of her. But why did she come back to work? It's not just a job for 'Just A Woman', is it? She's in it to make a difference and even though there will be many defeats, the occasional victory keeps her going.

And it's not all about downing thugs either. Most of the work of the gardaí is done on the quiet. A word here and a warning there. Young boys and girls are often given a chance when notebooks are kept closed. This isn't just a once-off. I'm a barman and I see trouble on the streets all the time. But it's late at night when you, the decent people, are asleep in your beds.

Take a drive around your city or town centre after 2am on any given weekend and you will see what our gardai have to face. Please do this. Do it for 'Just A Girl'. You'll be safe enough, once you stay in the car and keep the doors locked. And remember 'Just A Girl' didn't have that bubble to retreat back into when the going got tough.

There is a terrible and destructive binge-drinking culture in our country and, bad as the consequences are, the drug-taking is now epidemic. It usually takes official figures at least two years to catch up with the reality on the ground.

Attitudes can change in just a couple of years. Take it from me as absolutely true that a very high percentage of 14-16-year-olds are on drugs, mostly some form of marijuana. I would go so far as to say that in many areas of our country, a majority of kids have tried drugs.

And while you may say "hash isn't too bad", the stuff they sell now isn't grown by some hippie in a remote place near the coast.

Very often, the drugs are genetically modified. And the drugs aren't being sold by reputable pharmacists with the welfare of the client in mind. Most kids will go on to try something stronger.

Ireland is in the middle of the most deadly, pervasive attack on the health of our nation. Young lives are being ruined by the day and it's getting worse.

And it's 'Just A Girl' who will have to face the consequences, for us, who dial-a-cop.

'Just A Boy' threw his cap in the air when he graduated from The Garda Training College in Templemore. 'Just A Boy' was a Garda. Proudest day of his life.

It was a domestic. A battered wife needed him to go along with her to the old family home to collect some personal stuff. Another day in the life.

She was shot by her ex and the young lad who threw his cap in Templemore was murdered by him.

Tony Golden is his name and he died for Ireland last week in Omeath.

Just a dad.

Just a husband.

Just a Garda.

THE HUSBAND, WHO WAS
NOT THE FATHER, WAS A
CARPENTER BY THE NAME
OF JOSEPH. HIS WIFE,
THE MOTHER, WAS MARY.
THE CHILD WAS JESUS
AND HIS BIOLOGICAL FATHER
WAS GOD THE FATHER

53

Marriage Apartheid Is Illogical In A Church With A History Of Love

May 23, 2016

SOME stick with the old holiday company definition of the family. The one where the sun deals are for the mammy, the daddy, and the two kids. We had four and you'd nearly have to hand back a couple of the children to get a good deal.

Now that a year has passed since the passing of the marriage referendum, more babies are being born to gay couples. Mothers are conceiving in all sorts of wonderful ways. And isn't it lovely to see new life coming in to the world?

The parents were thrilled with their new baby. They had been childless. People came from far and wide to see the little boy God gave to the delighted couple.

There are three people in this family. Sort of. Four really if you include all the parties involved in the relationship quadrangle.

Let us say at the outset the family is very well thought of. Role models they are. All four of them and I know their story ever since I was small boy. The Catholic Church has very strict rules about what constitutes a family. I'm not sure if the family will fit in. The father was a third party. That's just for openers.

The methodology we are not too sure about. All I know is the mother became pregnant by a man without intercourse. Their story is out in the open for some time and was the subject of a bestseller. This story I am telling you here isn't exactly an exclusive but sometimes we forget old stories.

I had better name names. I suppose it's okay to do so when the story has been written up by others in the past.

The husband, who was not the father, was a carpenter by the name of Joseph. His wife, the mother, was Mary. The child was Jesus and his biological father was God the Father.

I know. I know. Isn't it desperate altogether the things people get up to? God help us.

The family is not even a proper family by the church definition. But what would the holy family know about holiness and religion?

I'm not even sure if the child would be entitled to receive baptism or take Holy Communion unless the situation was "regularised". In practice most priests turn a blind eye. They are good men. Christians even.

Here was my solution. Firstly the mother would have to divorce the father, the Joseph man father. Then she would marry the biological father. So it's all fixed up. Brilliant then amn't I? Should have been a theologian. I took advice from a friendly priest. My plan will fail.

The church doesn't recognise divorce and divorced people are not allowed to remarry in a Catholic church.

I gave up.

The rules need to be changed. Justice for all. There's nothing to be afraid of.

Many of you are good people who genuinely worry about what has been perceived as an attack on the status of the family as we once knew it to be, but I would ask you to open your hearts and your minds. Give the new families a chance. For the kids' sake.

The strictest of the Holier Than Thous only venture outside when they are protected by hard hats, like the ones the builders in the Village People wear. In case the skies fall down. When last I checked, the sky was still in situ.

The 500 or so gay people who were married since the referendum are the best campaigners of all. Neighbours and friends have been invited to the weddings and they saw for themselves just how normal and even ordinary the whole thing is. Saw the laughter. Saw the tears. Saw the love. So many I have met who voted No have changed their minds. The hard hats are hanging off a nail in the garden shed.

But there was no walking up the aisle, no beautiful words from the bible and no Communion.

The first 500 were left outside the church door. So sad. The devout gays know God loves them. Their prayers go straight to heaven. No rules can intercept the prayers of the faithful.

Here's the story of another high-profile family. One of their kids is gay and another married in a Catholic church. The mother and father have done so much to bring love and understanding to the peace process in the North. They bring people together from all walks of life and opened their home to all of the Irish.

President Mary and her husband Dr Martin have a courageous and articulate gay son. They stood by him and fought for him. The other McAleese kids are free to marry in a Catholic church but their brother is not.

Their story is replicated all over Ireland. I cannot make any sense out of the exclusion.

We have marriage apartheid in our church, a church with a history of extraordinary love and courage from priests and nuns who fought injustice and were tortured, imprisoned and martyred. Priest and nuns left home to fight for and minster to the excluded in South Africa during the apartheid regime.

You can canon law it all you like, but Irish men and Irish women are excluded from their church because they married the person they love. And their kids suffer because they weren't conceived in a bed. There is no other word. Apartheid it is.

As for the family we told you about at the top of the page, sad to say, their boy was crucified because he preached some sort of story about all of us loving each other.

THE BOY WHO CHANGES
LIVES HAS CHANGED MINE.
DONAL'S MESSAGE IS
EASY TO GET. LIVE. LIVE
AND MAKE THE MOST OF IT

54

Facing His Own Death, A Boy's Only Wish Was To Help Others

May 18, 2013

FIONNBAR Walsh told stories about his son's last day. "Do you know what he said to us? Just a couple of hours before he died. We took turns to sit with him. I was there at the bedside with his uncles. Donal woke up all of a sudden, and he looked up at us.

"'Ah lads,' he said, 'this is like a scene out of 'The Sopranos'."

Here's a kid on his death bed, trying to cheer up his loved ones. Donal Walsh not only prepared himself for death, but he prepared his family too.

Fionnbar said: "Sit in his shed for a while and read this."

He handed me a spiral notebook and inside were his 16-year-old son's notes, lines from songs and his own words.

Donal Walsh's shed was his den. A boy's hideout. His Kerry football jersey is pinned to the red timber wall. Next to his photographs of the Munster rugby team. In the middle is a table soccer game and Donal's racing bike is upside down and wheelless. His helmet is thrown in the corner. There's a small bottle of Lourdes water in the other corner and a massive drum kit sits silently in the middle of the red shed.

Another wall is given over to his friends. 'Love you Donal' is written everywhere. There are hearts in red marker. 'Don't go Dons'. His friends backed him up right to the end. Words of hope were stencilled by Donal on another wall. 'No stone unturned; Leave your fears behind!'

I was overcome, sitting alone in the red timber shed. We don't really live our lives at all, I thought. Those of us who have survived on the ledge, and those of us who just go from day to day without living every minute as if it were our last.

Donal's notebook is in his own neat handwriting.

"You gotta live every single day,

Like its the only one."

The boy who changes lives has changed mine. Donal's message is easy to get. Live. Live and make the most of it.

He spoke so passionately about suicide.

"So please, as a 16-year-old who has no say in his death sentence, who has no choice in the pain he is about to cause and who would take any chance at even a few more months on this planet, appreciate what you have, know that there are always other options and help is always there."

There's anger there, too, and that's how a dying 16-year-old boy will react. The notebook shows his true compassion for his fellow man. His love overcame the darkness. There's a kid's drawing in the notebook, of a coconut tree by a beach with birds and sun. On the tree are initials in a heart. We must not forget he was a young boy with a young boy's hopes and dreams. This is the context of Donal's statements on suicide. There was never a question of his lacking compassion for those who died so tragically.

"Everyone needs to feel loved," he wrote.

Yes, we do, young Donal. Yes, we do.

His stuff was still there. But he wasn't. Our sons played football against each other. Under 12. There was no football for Donal after that. Cancer came and he couldn't play. He was a classy player, willowy and silky, with a fierce passion for rugby and Gaelic football.

Fionnbar and Elma, Donal's lovely mother, brought me from the red shed.

What do you say: "Sorry for your troubles"? I was hoping they wouldn't think I was patronising them.

Late last night, Fionnbar texted me with my words to him when I came out of the red shed.

In the emotion I had forgotten.

"Jesus, there is a presence here beyond my understanding."

I meant it. I hope you don't think I'm making this up just for the sake of a good story. Because I'm not. Elma and Fionnbar felt it too. Their glance to each other and the expression in their eyes told it all. They spoke without words. Only couples who know each other's innermost thoughts can communicate in this way.

They told of how Donal had to be brought in a wheelchair to the set of the Brendan O'Connor show. He was very weak, but his plea to kids contemplating suicide will save lives. Donal wanted to save and save. So little time, and so much to do. Donal tried to get to see our President to enlist him in the cause, but the rigours of the journey would have meant he would not have been able to die at home.

Elma is calm. She has grace, good humour and a mother's practicality. We spoke of the funeral on the day after her son was laid to rest. "Donal would have been delighted with his send off," she said, "but a bit embarrassed too." The Munster team showed up and many of the Kerry team. The blue-and-white jerseys of Tralee RFC and Kerins O'Rahilly's GAA club were draped on his coffin.

They did a Haka for Donal and all his pals cried, especially the good-looking girls. "If Carlsberg did funerals . . ." I said without thinking and Elma laughed at the thought of it. She has become a passionate advocate for cancer care. "Surely a cure must be found," she pleads. Even now she was thinking of some other mother's son. "How did he find out?" I asked.

"He always knew," said Elma. "Donal forecast his death almost to the day. He was too intelligent to hide the truth from. He clammed up on us once when we held back. It was then we decided to tell him he had very little time."

It would be wrong to say Donal sailed through to the other side without any torment.

Earlier, on that last day, Donal woke up suddenly and said: "I'm not f***ing leaving. I'm going nowhere." Donal didn't want to die. But he was ready for death.

"What's on the other side Fr?" he asked of his parish priest, Fr Padraig Walsh .

"I don't know Donal, but it'll be a far better place with you in it.

"Are you afraid?" asked Fr Padraig.

"I'm not Fr, but I'm nervous."

Donal's notebook went through my head as his dad told the stories with word-perfect recall. I read the lines for him. It was his own paraphrasing of songs he liked by Nickleback.

"Each second counts cos there's no second try.

"Live your life like you'll never live it twice."

| 55 |

Donal Walsh's Last Video Is A Poem And A Prayer For The Living, The Forsaken And The Almost Broken

October 14, 2013

HE was there in the bright early summer in his own home at the foot of the mountains, on the edge of the sea by the banks of a canal.

In the place he loved best, shining out at us with his wavy brown hair, the handsome boyish face and the big, brown conker eyes.

Donal knew his life was ebbing fast.

He wanted to be told and his parents made sure. They knew him better than anyone. Knew he needed to know because Donal had things to do. Things to say. Quests to make and lives to save.

He was just a boy, like any other boy. So we must see him as one of his own gang. His own generation. Just a boy.

The new video clip produced by the HSE is very short but very powerful.

Donal's first raw interview hit home. Suicide rates dropped but time thieves away the strength of the message.

We forget.

Millions of images come at us every day. Space is filled in the editing suites in our heads and older stories make way for new clips.

The all too sad pattern is starting up again. Our teenagers are dying from suicide. Donal's father Fionbarr praises the courage shown by the parents of school girl Chloe Kinsella, who died by suicide last week in Limerick. "It was," he says, "like Donal was whispering on my shoulder. The priest said the family, in the depth of their grief, asked that the funeral would not be a glorification of suicide and they wanted the young people to choose to live life.

"Chloe's parents had the courage to continue the conversation Donal started."

Elma hopes her young lad's message will get through.

"When our teenagers see how weak Donal was physically and how his voice was beginning to go and how much of an effort it was for him, we hope they will listen. It took so much out of Donal to make the video. But he wanted to do it."

Donal wrote his epitaph through a journey of weeks rather than the years most of us get but he was also travelling to some sort of a state of grace.

Maybe it's just me and part of our innate human longing for some sort of sign there is another life, a hereafter. A place to meet those we have lost or those we are leaving behind. This is the big question of our time, or any other age.

Donal's thinking was clear, even if the frail body was giving up on him.

It was as if Donal had help from a higher power and that in some way your God and mine was speaking through the teenager from Blennerville.

And so we have formed the opinion that young Donal's last poem was made half-way between heaven and here.

56

Learning The Secrets Of Mary Catherine, Bringing Joy To Her Family For 100 Years

September 15, 2014

MARY CATHERINE has lived here all her life. One hundred years in the same house, and her family have farmed in Chancellorsland since 1750.

Tara, the silky border collie, jumps up for fun in the autumn sun. The Tipperary hurling flag butterflies in the warm breeze. The wavy fields are almost ready for the last cut of hay. The farm is a mile from Emly, a perfect Tidy Towns winning village in the heartland of Tipperary. It's the kind of rural heaven, where you could easily live forever.

Mary Catherine greets us at the door. The Bean an Tí has the bright eyes of the young girl and her walk is lively and upright. You'd love to plant a kiss on her silvery curls. She wears a lacy white blouse, ironed by herself, and a smart skirt. The glasses are taken off her for the photograph

"Will you leave on the cardigan?" asks her daughter Esther who enjoys her mother no end. "I will not," replies Mary Catherine, "Sure I'm dressed lovely."

We enquire how she got on at the gambling. "I play cards six nights a week all around the area and sure it keeps me going." She's not gone on the Progressive 45 though. "It's a mean game where you hit and rip all around you."

Last week she won "a good few hundred. I can read their cards without having to look."

Her son John, a retired teacher, his wife Anne and their children are very good to Mary Catherine. They live next door and

Mary Catherine knocks great sport out of the grandchildren. Daughter Ann is on her way from Limerick for the celebrations. Esther pours the tea in the homely living room where we are eating an apple pie made by the woman of the house. The room where she was born is just off the living room. There's history here.

She tells of the IRA bringing informers to the Sinn Fein courts through their fields and of nights when her mother fed The Flying Column who were on the run from the murdering Black And Tans. Mary Catherine keeps up with the events of the day. She believes Ireland is on the way back to prosperity and is a strong supporter of Fine Gael even since her family took the Collins' side in the Civil War.

The times were tough but the only lines on her face are carved from laughter. Mary Catherine was feisty and she still is.

"While the men were talking in the kitchen I drove off in the tractor and ploughed a field. I must have only been 18. I was an only child and it was tough on me to get going. I used to sneak out the window to go to dances. I always said if I had a family of my own I wouldn't be too strict on them."

Pat died when he was 53 after a very long illness. "He was a vegetable for the last year." Pat, a fine looking man, was the love of her life. I ask Mary Catherine if she ever thought about marrying again.

"Aren't you very inquisitive? I am fine the way I am. There's no one to put me in or out. I can do what I like."

John tells us: "She milked the cows by hand and worked as hard as any man."

"The neighbours were great," says Mary Catherine. In comes the postman with a shoal of cards and a bun. Emly is a place where people care and take care.

A specialist advised her to go in to a home a few years back when Mary Catherine was very ill. She was indignant and let the specialist know exactly what she thought of his proposal.

We are here after a chance meeting with our old friend Tadhg

O'Meara at a faraway airport. I was here to find out her secret. For you, and for me.

"Freda died suddenly at 40, from a stroke."

Mary Catherine was devastated, "but I just got on with it." Freda and Pat are very much in her thoughts today.

Mary Catherine says five novenas in bed every morning and she has an especially strong devotion to the Sacred Heart. "I accept all that happened," she says.

"I have a bowl of porridge and home-made brown bread every morning." Her favourite dinner? "Bacon and cabbage." She still cooks and bakes and Mary Catherine takes a walk of a mile and a half through the farm she kept going in tough times.

There's so much more to be written about this lady who is one of the transition generation who put family first and reared today's Irish women to stand on their own two feet.

We said goodbye with a kiss and a firm hug. For some reason my own worries didn't seem so overwhelming.

There was one last glance in the car mirror.

Mary Catherine Buckley was smiling serenely, as she looked out over the silky grass of Chancellorsland from the front door of her own home, where she brought so much joy 100 years ago today.

WE GET THEM IN DROVES. THEY HAVE NO NOTION OF BUYING ANYTHING. ONE LAD EVEN ASKED ME IF IT WOULD BE ALRIGHT FOR HIMSELF AND HERSELF TO EAT THEIR SANDWICHES IN THE PUB

57

Tyre Kickers And Cheapskates Can Keep Me Entertained But They Drive The Mother Mad

July 21, 2014

THE car salesman tells me he gets them as well. This is the peak season for the visits of the cheap people who window shop in our pub. They visit the car salesman in January, his busiest time. Tyre kickers he calls them.

The husband and wife take a drive about, usually on a Saturday, and in they go to the showroom. Every car is looked at and a thousand questions are asked like 'how's she on the juice?' and 'who owned her last?' The man usually gives the tyre a tap with his shoe as if to check the pressure. The day out it's called.

We get them in droves. They have no notion of buying anything. One lad even asked me if it would be alright for himself and herself to eat their sandwiches in the pub.

"Fine," I said, just for the fun of it. I began to tell them about all my overheads. "Did you know that publicans have to pay a tax on pint glasses?"

It's true, we do. I wasn't winding them up. The plan was to make them feel guilty and then after a series of subtle hints they would be shamed into buying a drink.

The plan didn't work.

"Awful blackguarding that taxing people for glasses," said she. Then he takes two mugs the size of saucepans out of a bag and asks would I mind filling them up with boiling water.

"No bother at all," says I, "and are ye alright for tea bags?" knowing well the mother would be back in the pub in a few minutes and the steam would come out her ears.

The mother did come back in and for a minute I thought she was going to get the brush to them. But then when she calmed just a bit, over she goes to the cheapskates with her fist clenched and her lips going purple, which is a sure sign she's in a right tear.

In the meantime, he asks: "Have ye any oul books ye've read yourselves wrote by the father. We're gatherin' dem for the Bazaar for The Foreign Missions."

The mother tells the two she has to charge them corkage on the packet of biscuits they've just taken out for the last part of their picnic. The lady asked my mother if she had any souvenirs. The mother signed a beer mat for them. Then the lady asks the mother: 'What age are you now?' The mother is losing her reason at this stage. She replies: "I'm the same age as I was this time last year, only a year older."

I tell the tyre kickers the mother has just turned 107. "Isn't she very fresh for her age all the same," compliments the nice lady with her mouth half-full of biscuits. Her husband whispers to me: 'Has she all her marbles?' The mother who can hear the grass growing in the family farm in Knocknagoshel, some 20 miles away, gets every word.

The mother is very annoyed by now and she says: "In all my 107 years, I've never met anyone as tight as the two of ye." The two get a desperate fit of laughing, as if the mother is joking or a cracked old dear or a bit of character.

They make for the door and I say: "Call again the next time ye are back in town." The mother passes a remark, something along the lines of 'I reared an eejit.'

The worst part is all the questions. It's not so bad answering questions when someone buys a drink and the tyre kickers never seem to tire of enquiries.

Last summer we had a glut of tyre kickers, what with the fine weather. By late September I was gone demented.

This lad who asked for a glass of tap water asked me a million questions and I answer them all politely. I heard a story of the hotelier on the Ring of Kerry who used to charge €2 for a glass of tap water. He called it draft still. I'm not sure if that story is true or not but I hope it is.

The lad asks "for a few knobs of ice, if it's no trouble." I oblige.

"But wasn't your father a fierce brainy man. Did he leave much after him?"

"Oh, he did indeed," says I, wondering if I'd get much jail time for doing him in with the ice tongs.

So instead of killing him I opt for torture. Out I go to the deep freeze and in I come with a frozen roast of beef. "There's the father's brain," I say. The man goes pale. He gets up off the stool he has been parked on for an hour and is about to leave, but I'm not finished with him.

"He was so smart," I continue, "the doctors took out his brain and when they were finished their tests, they gave it back to us and we froze it."

The foreigners are nearly as bad as our own lads. There was the night when the bar was buzzing for our summer pub theatre (Tuesdays and Thursdays) and six French people took up the best seats. They bought just one glass of Guinness between the six of them. The French passed around the glass. Each one took a sip and licked their lips. Two hours they stayed and, as our pub is small enough, a good few real customers came in and left because there was nowhere to sit.

Sometimes you have to laugh.

"I'd swear," said the mother, "that the French crowd gave a few staggers when they were going out the front door."

WE HAVE THIS THEORY HERE IN ROME THAT IF YOU ELECT AN OLD MAN AND IF HE TURNS OUT TO BE A BAD POPE, HE WILL NOT BE AROUND LONG ENOUGH TO CAUSE MAJOR DAMAGE TO THE CHURCH

58

The Concept Of Infallibility Would Pose No Difficulties For A Female Pope

February 18, 2013

THE cardinals will meet in Rome in the middle of next month for the papal election. It normally takes a few days, what with the usual canvassing and horse-trading.

It's no different to your average county council election: "Can you get a new roof for my basilica? And is there any chance you could fill in that pothole outside the convent before one of the smaller nuns falls in and gets drowned? And where's the 'Father Ted' box set you promised me?"

It's well within the bounds of possibility that the new pope will be elected on St Patrick's Day. Maybe we might even have an Irish pope on the day that's in it. Pope Patrick might be the new man's name. The cardinals might even elect an Irish woman like, say, Mary McAleese who's a theologian and was the most popular head of state in the world when she was our President.

But in this time of election fever, we can exclusively report there will not be a woman pope. Under no circumstances. Whatsoever.

A source close to the Vatican revealed as much in an exclusive interview.

The source is a cardinal, and a Vatican insider of long standing. We go back a long way. Back to the time when I was a spud peeler in his nephew's chipper in a town near the sea. The cardinal was frank.

"Sure, how could you put up with a woman pope?" he scoffed. "There you'd be lying down on a sofa that was once owned by Michelangelo and in comes Il Papa with: 'What are you doing stretched out there watching Serie A when there's work to be done?'"

Then His Excellency lets out a little shriek, like he was goosed. It seems His Munificence was standing on a ventilation grid and a blast of sibilant hot air blew up his cassock. Some Like it Hot.

I suggest Alex Ferguson for pope. The Manchester United manager is not a Catholic, but he can switch over in a free transfer. All it takes is a bucket of water for the baptism. And no one knows the difference between Protestantism and Catholicism anyway.

The cardinal disagrees. "Yes, Sir Alex has the leadership skills, but at 71 he's far too young."

I ask His Wonderfulness why it is that new popes are so old.

"Simple," he says. "We have this theory here in Rome that if you elect an old man and if he turns out to be a bad pope, he will not be around long enough to cause major damage to the church. If we pick some guy in his 50s, he's there forever and the church could be destroyed. Look at what 20 years of continuous Fianna Fail rule did to your country."

I had to admit there was some sense in that argument.

Your correspondent lives in a house containing three daughters and just the one wife. Over the course of a good many years I have become a feminist, if not by inclination, then by instruction and immersion.

We revisit the vexed question of a woman pope.

"Is it not a disgrace," I ask, "that women are treated as inferior beings within the Catholic church?"

The cardinal's voice becomes more animated. He's at the level of three tenors.

"My child, you must open your eyes and look at the world around you. I am no misogynist. Indeed, just between ourselves and the fresco, I have two bambinos with a lovely buxom lass in Napoli going back to the time when the moon hit my eye like a big pizza pie.

"But we have decided it is best to keep women out of the running of the church. They make lists, you see. And they are not satisfied until all the items on the list are ticked. Change must be slow or not at all. In the Vatican the man wears the dress.

"Though I must say, in defence of women, that the concept of infallibility is one with which they are readily familiar."

Old misogynist that he is, he chuckles heartily at his own witticism. Today is February 18, the 530th anniversary of the death of Martin Luther. I suggest to the cardinal that it is high time for another reformation, what with all these sex abuse cover-ups, the silencing of dissenting voices in the church and the absence of a viable strategy on contraception in countries that are riddled with Aids.

I tell the cardinal that the prohibition of women priests is simply nonsensical.

"I will quote John Lennon for you," says His Eminence, who is well used to batting for the establishment and readily drifts into the safety of dogma and prepared script.

"Lennon it was who said: 'As usual, there is a great woman behind every idiot.'

"Luther was married to Catherine von Bora, and what, my son, was her profession?"

Before I could answer, the cardinal had answered his own question.

"She was a nun. Yes, a nun. A reverend mother. And it was Catherine who gave him that list of grievances he nailed to the church door," he said.

"She started the Reformation, and the church is still splitting up all these years on. And do you think a woman priest could keep the gossip she picks up in confession to herself?"

I remind His Excellency that the Virgin Mary was a woman.

THE PAIN EBBS AND
FLOWS AND I KNOW MAM,
BEING THE PRACTICAL
COUNTRYWOMAN WOMAN
THAT SHE IS, WOULD BE
SAYING: "CUT IT OUT AND GET
ON WITH IT. SHOP FACE, BILL"

59

Today Is The Day Of The Two Marys, I Cannot Let My Mam Go

August 15, 2016

HOLY Mary is revered in Ireland and the Hail Mary is our favourite prayer. Today is the Feast of the Assumption, the 15th of August, the day some of us believe Holy Mary was taken into heaven.

The fifteenth has always been a big day out. Féile Mhuire 'sa bhFomhar it was known as in the days when Irish was the countrywide vernacular. That's the festival of our Lady of the Harvest.

The Pattern Day, it's called now. The Pattern probably grew out of the banning of churches and Masses back in the days of the Penal Laws. Even the English couldn't burn down the sky. So we met out in the open.

There's a touch of the pagan about the day out that the English and the church could never tame. The Irish, as ever, managed to make a piss-up out of a holy day. The Synod of Tuam in 1660 decreed that "dancing, flute-playing, bands of music, riotous revels and other abuses in visiting wells and other holy places are forbidden".

The Pattern in Tallaght was suppressed due to "drunkenness and debauchery" in 1874. The wild country people of Tallaght kept the party going with a visit to the grave of the toper piper Burley O' Toole.

Burley's last wish was that there would be fighting and drinking round his last resting place on the fifteenth.

Today was the day us townies used to thumb out to Ballybunion to check out the last of the old boys who took their yearly dip in the Atlantic. There they'd be, gingerly facing into the waves, in their second-skin long johns.

A nurse told me you'd nearly have to hire a big game hunter, well used to skinning his prey, to prize the long johns off the old boys when they died. The onesies were worn winter and summer and the dip in the sea was a wash for man and underpants.

Up then with the fifteenths to the town of Ballybunion for a feed of periwinkles – and the saltiness drove them mad for porter.

For many who were the slaves of the jailers known as the cows, it was their only day off in summer.

The day is still celebrated but the crowds are well down. The Irish have pagan days every day now.

We used to go to sports meetings in the villages on the fifteenth. I was beaten in the under-14 100 yards by a lad with a wife and two children. And you thought the Olympics were dodgy.

The holy side is still kept up at the holy wells on Pattern Day. But what of Holy Mary and is she still the queen of Ireland?

I know there are many reasons for the Christian split, including the fact that the wives of the syphilitic psychopath Henry VIII only ever lived up to his expectations when they died.

But it seems the main reasons we have Protestants and Catholics is down to a dispute over the veracity of the Immaculate Conception.

I would say "so what?" It matters not how Jesus was conceived, but how he lived and died.

Strange, isn't it, then that more than 2,000 years on from Mary's assumption, the Catholic bosses, who fought wars for the honour of the Virgin Mary, will not allow women to become priests.

Our default prayer when we were kids was the Hail Mary – and what a lovely, simple prayer it is.

To this day, I find myself rattling off Hail Marys in my head when I'm in trouble or when I'm worried about family or friends.

The Irish always had great reverence for Holy Mary.

We were a conquered nation of the dispossessed and who better to pray to than a refugee lady whose son was state-murdered before her very eyes.

There were more personal reasons too. My grandmother died in childbirth when my mother was only three years old.

My mother was Mary and so when her own mother died, she adopted Holy Mary as her mother.

I remember sitting on my Mam's lap in our tiny kitchen upstairs and she was teaching me the Hail Mary.

I am a believer. I believe Holy Mary was a good woman and a good mother and a brave mother, who risked her own life to care for the body of her dead son.

I know there are terrible happenings in the world but Holy Mary is not responsible for the evil in men's hearts. The poor pray to her for help and even that very act is a statement of support for justice and humanity. There is comfort in the comfort praying. We know that we are not alone and that a mother's love is always there, as I found out when I lost my way.

Holy Mary showed us how to love and live and how to forgive. And I really do believe that she was brought to Heaven when she died, whatever or wherever that may be.

I'm writing this piece on the fourteenth. When I started to write, I was fine. Decided to stay away from grief but then the recollection of these very days from last year came back.

Today is the first anniversary of my Mam's passing. I refuse to cry. Don't know why.

I cannot let go of my mother. I must keep her memory and the sight of her in the here and now.

The pain ebbs and flows and I know Mam, being the practical countrywoman woman that she is, would be saying: "Cut it out and get on with it. Shop face, Bill."

But I can't. Not able.

It's as if I was being disloyal to my Mam by letting go. The memory of her might fade away and I might forget how she sounded or what her face looked like.

I can hear her now. I tap away on the laptop, but it's more the tone of her voice I hear than the actual words. She is still with us.

But what will I do to get over the loss when the pain comes back again?

I will say a Hail Mary, that's what I'll do.

Just like I did when I was a small boy, in our tiny kitchen, up over the din of the pub before Mam went downstairs to work and I had her all to myself.

Acknowledgements

THANKS to PJ Cunningham of Ballpoint Press who gave me my first column and is now my publisher. Joe Coyle did a wonderful job designing the book and award-winning photographer Mark Condren always makes me look prettier than I really am.

I owe a huge debt to the excellent editorial team in the *Irish Independent* for minding me for 16 years.

Finally thanks to my family for putting up with me.